# FIREFIGHTERS

Larry Shapiro

This edition first published in 2003 by MBI Publishing Company, Galtier Plaza, Suite 200, 380 Jackson Street, St. Paul, MN 55101-3885 USA

MBI titles are also available at discounts in bulk quantity for industrial or sales-promotional use. For details write to Special Sales Manager at Motorbooks International Wholesalers & Distributors, Galtier Plaza, Suite 200, 380 Jackson Street, St. Paul, MN 55101-3885 USA.

Library of Congress Cataloging-in-Publication Data

Shapiro, Larry, 1958-
    Firefighters/by Larry Shapiro
        p. c.m.
    Includes Index.
    ISBN 0-7603-1494-2 (pbk. : alk. paper)
        1. Fire extinction—Juvenile literature. 2. Fire fighters—Juvenile literature. I. Title.

    TH 9148.S49 2003
    363.37—dc21                              2003048731


Edited by Leah Noel
Designed by Mandy Iverson

Printed in China

**On the front cover:** Two firefighters man an attack line with full protective gear. Most modern firefighters utilize helmets, Nomax hoods, gloves, self contained breathing apparatus along with bunker pants and coats to provide total encapsulation for protection against burns. Here, the nozzleman is assisted by another firefighter off the engine.

**On the frontispiece:** After going through several training rotations in an abandoned house, two firefighters with a hose line make sure that the remaining fire doesn't get out of hand and endanger the adjacent properties while they let the structure burn to the ground. Neighboring homes and environmental concerns about the air and hazardous materials have greatly curtailed the ability of local fire departments to burn down abandoned and donated homes for training purposes. When they do get the needed approvals, the training often becomes a community event, drawing large crowds that are attracted to the sight of a raging fire.

**On the title page:** It's not possible to win every firefight. Three firefighters train a hose line on the smothering remains of a horse stable silhouetted by floodlights used to illuminate the area for safety. Small lights mounted to their helmets offer additional light.

**On the introduction page:** This image, taken in 1979, speaks volumes about tradition. The well-worn coat and helmet represent a seasoned firefighter from Chicago's elite Snorkel Squad 1. Signs of heat and smoke exposure together have created a helmet that was worn with great pride, perhaps even invoking envy from other firefighters.

**On the back cover:** Each fire department is tasked with staffing its companies within budget constraints. The majority of the firefighters pictured here, as members of the Prospect Heights Fire Protection District in Illinois, are career firefighters with other departments. They provide staffing for Prospect Heights on days that they are not assigned to their full-time departments. Here they have just completed a day of live fire training.

**Author Bio**

Larry Shapiro is a photographer whose experience spans more than 26 years. His portfolio includes work for private, commercial, and corporate clients, but his passion lays in his all consuming love of the fire service and all things motorized. During his career, he has provided photographic services for multiple fire truck manufacturers including American LaFrance, Emergency One, Grumman, HME, LTI, Luverne, Pierce, Pirsch, Seagrave, and Sutphen, plus heavy truck builders Freightliner, Oshkosh, Sterling, and Western Star, in the form of advertisements, calendars, and sales literature.

Larry has also provided photography for several books and calendars that were written by others in addition to authoring and illustrating eight books to date. His previous titles with MBI Publishing Company include, Aerial Fire Trucks, Cranes in Action, Fighting Fire Trucks, Hook & Ladders, Pumpers: Workhorse Fire Engines, Special Police Vehicles, and Tow Trucks in Action.

Larry lives with his wife and three sons in the suburbs of Chicago.

# CONTENTS

# DEDICATION

The task of protecting lives and property in America is the responsibility of police, fire, and emergency medical service (EMS) personnel. Every day these individuals deal with routine, mundane, exciting, tragic, heroic, fulfilling, and disappointing tasks. They understand that people young and old rely on their expertise and training for assistance with minor and serious medical issues, automobile accidents, foul or suspicious odors, fires large and small, as well as any number of unknown requests. Each time they respond there is the remote possibility that they may be called upon to intervene in a situation that could involve life-or-death decisions for the citizens that they have vowed to protect or for themselves.

According to U.S. Fire Administration statistics, 102 firefighters died in 2002. Full-time career firefighters accounted for 37 of the deaths, and the balance came from the ranks of volunteer, seasonal, and part-time firefighters. The number of firefighter deaths in 2001 peaked at 446, with the horrors of September 11 accounting for 343 of those lost lives. In the last 25 years, 1992 saw the fewest firefighter deaths with the loss of 75 dedicated individuals. In 2001, 228 law enforcement officers died in the line of duty, a figure that includes the 70 who lost their lives on September 11. As of June 2002, 68 police and other law enforcement officers had lost their lives while protecting others.

Tragically, more emergency personnel die every month. As with any loss of life, families, friends, and co-workers experience the repercussions from each loss. This book is dedicated to all emergency workers that make the ultimate sacrifice in the pursuit of their passions: protecting lives and property and helping others.

## The firefighter's prayer:

*When I'm called to duty God,*
*wherever flames may rage,*
*grant me the strength to save a life*
*whatever be its age*

*Help me to embrace a little child*
*before it is too late*
*or save an older person*
*from the horror of that fate*

*Enable me to be alert*
*to hear the weakest shout*
*and quickly and efficiently*
*put the fire out*

*I want to fill my calling Lord*
*and give the best in me*
*to guard my every neighbor and*
*protect his property*

*And if according to your will*
*I am to lose my life,*
*God bless with your protecting hand*
*my children and my wife*

*—Author unknown*

# ACKNOWLEGMENTS

I would like to take this opportunity to mention several people that were instrumental in providing assistance that enabled me to write this book. Several firefighters offered their time to sit down and talk about life on the job, recalling stories and personal feelings toward a profession that is full of such rich tradition that it lures individuals from all walks of life. I hope that by listing their names individually, they will understand my gratitude for their help.

As always, the list is alphabetical, lest anyone feel that I am playing favorites. Thanks to Robert J. (Bob) Barraclough (for all of the numerical statistics); New York City firefighter Kevin Kroth, FDNY Rescue 1; Brian Johnson, paid-on-call firefighter for the Northfield (Illinois) Fire Rescue Department, career firefighter/paramedic for the Schaumburg (Illinois) Fire Department, and field instructor at the Illinois Fire Service Training Institute (IFSTI); Norm Johnson, retired battalion chief for the Glenview (Illinois) Fire Department; Rick Kolomay, lieutenant for the Schaumburg (Illinois) Fire Department and field instructor at IFSTI; Ray Orozco, deputy district chief at the Chicago Fire Department Sixth District, field instructor at IFSTI, and adjunct professor at Harold Washington College, department of fire science; Scott Sutherland, career firefighter for the Schaumburg (Illinois) Fire Department; Lieutenant Tony Tarabocchia, FDNY Rescue 1; and Tom Whitaker, paid-on-call firefighter/paramedic for the Northfield (Illinois) Fire Rescue Department, career firefighter/paramedic for the Wheeling (Illinois) Fire Department, and field instructor at IFSTI.

I always appreciate the comments, support, questions, and criticisms that I receive from friends and acquaintances in the fire service with regards to the books that I have written to date. I consider each encounter that I have during visits to fire departments and while interacting with professionals around the country valuable to my ongoing education on the fire service since I am not a firefighter. Jumping at every chance to sample different opportunities, such as tillering a rig for the first time or entering a burning building, continues to stir feelings of jealousy that I have since I never tested for a department. I have great personal respect for all those that have entered the fire service and carry on the traditions of generations.

I'd also like to thank my family, who is extremely important to me and continues to be supportive of my interests. Most of all, my wife Dorothy always encourages me to pursue my dreams and offers the strength and support that I need. I am blessed to have her as my partner.

# INTRODUCTION

Since the time fire became a part of man's existence, its benefits and detriments to our quality of life have been irrefutable. As the destructive ability of fire has threatened lives and property since the first civilizations, man continually has been forced to defend against it. Fighting fires has been a noble endeavor throughout the world and has, over time, become a passionate pursuit for those who have chosen it as a full-time career, a part-time endeavor, or by acting as a volunteer.

Although the roots of fighting fires is rich in history dating back to the early Romans, *Firefighters* is a look into modern firefighting so that readers can be educated about this fascinating call to arms that attracts so many individuals and families in the United States. Quite often, second, third, and even fourth generations of families decide to follow in the footsteps of relatives who dedicate their professional or private lives to fighting fires and risk their lives to protect the lives and properties of friends, neighbors, and complete strangers.

Throughout this book, I refer to the distinction between full-time or career firefighters and those that volunteer. As recently as the year 2000, National Fire Protection Association (NFPA) statistics in the United States set the total number of firefighters around 1,064,150. It may come as a surprise to many that 75 percent of these, or some 777,350, are not full-time firefighters, but students, blue-collar and white-collar workers, self-employed individuals, professional or unemployed workers, or stay-at-home parents.

Acting as a volunteer or part-time firefighter, therefore, is far more common nationwide than having the ability to choose firefighting as a full-time career. The question of whether or not many of these part-time firefighters would retain full-time positions if they were offered goes without saying.

In the following chapters, I'll try and give some insight into many of the reasons for pursuing this dangerous, exciting, and extremely fulfilling profession. In addition, I'll cover the many changes that have been instituted throughout the fire service, making the pursuit of a career as a firefighter harder, of less interest, or out of reach for many.

You will learn about the daily lives and duties of firefighters, what their training is like, what their personal gear is, and read accounts of their active responses and chilling moments. Big city paid departments and smaller volunteer departments will offer different, and at the same time similar, insights into the career that has lured many people from safer, higher-paying jobs into the service of running into buildings just as most people are running out. You'll learn what it takes to become a firefighter and perhaps be able to judge whether you have what it takes to make the grade.

In a post-September 11 era, I'll also try and convey why so many, especially among the ranks of New York City Fire Department (FDNY), continue to regard this profession as *"still the best job in the world."*

# CHAPTER 1
# A Modern Day Firefighter

With ice formed all over his bunker coat and covering the face shield of his helmet, a protective hood shielding his head, and a cup of coffee from the Salvation Army Canteen in his hand, this firefighter can only be thinking one thing: It just doesn't get any better than this.

LEFT: For the most part, gender barriers in the fire service were broken down in the last two decades. Now most men in the fire service accept working with and relying on women as firefighters, but there will always be those with outdated customs that inherently look only to other men. Even as attitudes change, women may have to put forth an extra effort in what has long been a man's culture full of intense physical requirements.

RIGHT: Local civil defense (CD) or emergency services disaster agency (ESDA) groups that volunteer for many types of events sometimes supplement full-time and volunteer fire departments. Several members of the local CD handle a line at this extra alarm lumberyard fire in 1977 in Skokie, Illinois.

Firefighters, and firefighting, have changed drastically in the United States since the early days when wagons pulled by horses or volunteer townsmen rattled down cobblestone streets carrying large barrels of water, which then was pumped onto a raging fire. The growth of a nation forced larger cities to organize fire departments and pay for protection. Then the industrial era hit, bringing both improvements in building structures (more steel, less wood) and firefighting equipment (more trucks, no horses). Improvements in technology, firefighting techniques, and building codes fueled even more changes over the decades, as did the integration of women into department ranks in the latter part of the twentieth century.

Now in the early years of the twenty-first century, improvements in technology continue to change the role of firefighters as they use more high-tech equipment and require more specialized training than ever before. The terrorist attacks of September 11, 2001, also emphasized how the firefighter's role now encompasses much more than just protecting people in burning buildings, tending to medical needs, and responding to hazardous material spill—they also now have to be concerned with biological threats.

### It's Not the Same Job Anymore
In decades past, fighting fires—or attacking the red devil, putting the wet stuff on the red stuff, and a host of other clichés—fully described what the job was about. Fortunately for the population at large, but to the detriment of the thrill-seeking, fire-loving firefighters, there has been a significant and steady decline in fire duty in the last 25 years. National Fire Protection Association (NFPA) data from 1977, for example, reported

more than 1,000,000 structure fires, an excess of 500,000 vehicle fires, and more than 1,600,000 outside fires. By 2001, the numbers had dropped to about 500,000 structure fires, a little more than 350,000 vehicle fires, and just over 800,000 outside fires. The numbers represent a 50 percent drop in structure fires and outside fires, while vehicle fires dropped roughly 30 percent—not good news for those thousands of firefighters who long for the excitement of action.

Instead of only responding to fire calls, firefighters now also have the responsibility of emergency medical service (EMS) providers. For many departments, medical responses currently represent nearly 70 percent of their emergency requests and are constantly increasing, while fighting fires and performing other duties are down roughly 30 percent, according to the NFPA. The very existence of a large majority of fire departments today relies on incorporating EMS into their doctrine. This emphasis on providing medical help is a discouragement for some who entered the fire service to fight fires. It remains a delicate issue, but it is a fact of modern-day life. Over and over again, firefighters can be heard to say that constantly running EMS calls is not what they originally signed on for. But even many of the old timers agree that the need for some medical training is imperative for firefighters.

There was a time, before the modern integration of EMS into the fire service, when firefighters, who were significantly greater in numbers and proximity than the EMS providers, would arrive

In York City, Pennsylvania, volunteers bolster the career firefighters. They train together and work side by side. The only way to tell them apart is by the color of their turnout gear, with black representing the volunteers. In 1999, the company received these two new American LaFrance rigs, a heavy rescue unit and a tractor-drawn aerial.

on the scene to find an injured person that they were not trained to assist. Helplessly, the firefighters were able to do little but stand by and await the arrival of the EMS crew, a situation that was extremely awkward and embarrassing in front of witnesses and family members. In many areas, particularly in large cities, this

The pride of volunteerism is evident in this photo depicting members of the Pitt Township Fire Department from Harpster, Ohio. Representing a wide range of ages, the volunteers posed here with their new Pierce pumper/tanker that was delivered in 2002. The chief has the most years of service to date and has been with the department since 1967, while the newest member has been on the department for slightly more than two years.

RIGHT: The well-worn leather helmet and turnout coat on this firefighter signal many years of service. With a determined look on his face, this veteran firefighter works to finish his assigned task so that he can offer further assistance to other firefighters.

With the temperatures below freezing, water turns to ice wherever it lands, as evidenced by this firefighter's ice-encrusted helmet and turnout gear. The building that is visible in the background has been totally destroyed by the blaze.

problem was one impetus that led to the initial basic first-aid training for firefighters who were assigned to fire suppression duties. This training allowed them to become first responders for minor medial emergencies.

EMS training in some fire departments is mandatory, either to the emergency medical technician (EMT) level or to that of a full paramedic. In most cases, this additional training and the added responsibilities that go along with it, translates into a higher base pay than for those firefighters who do not undergo the added instruction. To become an EMT, firefighters must complete roughly 100 hours of training to be able to perform many medical procedures. A paramedic receives the most training, six more months than an EMT, and is certified to administer narcotics, monitor telemetry, and provide defibrillation to restart a heart that has stopped beating.

Other than responding to medical calls, firefighters in many areas now often respond less to working fires than to automatic fire alarm activations, most of which are false alarms. Newer cities with strong building codes prevent many fires through better construction, automatic suppression systems, and early detection through smoke and heat sensors. Because multiple false alarms can keep firefighters from responding to a true emergency, some fire departments charge those businesses, or residences that have had numerous false alarms.

Since September 11, the fire service and its lure have changed for many. Cities with dense population centers, tourist areas, or major events have become potential targets for terrorists, and the fire service is the first line of defense for the public. This reality was painfully evident with the rash of anthrax scares in October 2001. Fire departments quickly became the first responders to these incidents, being tasked with coming into contact with the unknown substance and

performing initial testing. Only upon fire department recognition of a suspicious substance did the FBI or the military come in to handle the follow-up investigation. In these and any other instance in which anthrax was mentioned, including domestic situations, protocol dictated that fire departments should enter first to assess the danger and provide the "all-clear" before police should enter. Normally, protocol dictates that police enter first in many situations so that officers can secure the scene and firefighters' safety.

The growing number of hazardous materials emergencies has increased the need for specialization within many fire departments. Other types of situations have also prompted the need for specific expertise including training on below grade rescues (people trapped underground in cave-ins, holes, or tunnels), high angle rescues (people high above the ground, such as those stranded on tall scaffolds or wilderness mountainsides), or responses related to the threats of urban terrorism under the new umbrella of homeland security.

Another factor that has served to change the job of a firefighter is technology. Although largely viewed as a positive influence, the increased use of technology can be a detriment within this tradition-laced, hands-on profession that requires constant learning. Just as in a traditional work environment, the growth of computers and e-mail communications has in many cases reduced the old-fashioned, face-to-face contact that promotes unity, camaraderie, and strong bonds between people.

Some of the younger firefighters rely on this technology for answers and solutions instead of working with more seasoned co-workers who can provide answers based on successful personal experiences or mistakes. Reading an account of a search that failed or a fire attack that went wrong cannot take the place of an eye-to-eye conversation with someone that was there. As with any aspect of the job, many firefighters feel there needs to be an appropriate mixture of technology along with old-fashioned mentoring.

Regardless of these changes in duty and technology, modern-day firefighters do share commonalities with the decades of American firefighters who came before them. For one, just as in the days of old, most firefighters in the United States do their duty on a volunteer basis. According to statistics from the NFPA, full-time paid fire departments make up approximately only seven percent of the total number of fire departments in the United States. In 2000, the number of career or fully paid fire departments was 1,878. The rest of the reported 24,476 departments consisted of 1,407 that were mostly paid (more than 50 percent full-time paid personnel), 3,845 that were mostly volunteer (more than 50 percent volunteer personnel), and 19,224 that were completely volunteer.

Volunteer firefighters may receive no money, may be paid for a specific block of time that they are on-call, or paid a small stipend for the calls they respond to. Regardless of their compensation, volunteer and part-time firefighters go through rigorous training, answer emergency

It's no easy task climbing a steep aerial ladder to the roof of a four-story building with air packs on your back, an ax in your belt, and a pike pole in one hand. Some ladders are easier to climb than others, as the width of the ladder sections and the rungs under foot can affect how quickly they can be climbed. This particular ladder, a five-section, 135-foot, E-ONE aerial, is set at a fairly steep angle.

For many firefighters, there is little that compares to the adrenaline rush that comes from responding to an emergency call. With the lights flashing and the siren wailing, you speed through intersections and weave around traffic as everyone scrambles to get out of the way.

calls with the same fervor as career firefighters, and often help raise money to keep their department's equipment up to date. In contrast to career firefighters who derive their income from the fire service, volunteers are people performing a service to their communities solely out of a sense of the need to protect their neighbors, their community, and themselves from the ravage of fire or other traumatic events. These committed people safeguard lives and property in areas where there is no full-time, career fire department.

A major fire on Long Island requires mutual aid from many departments, most of which are staffed by volunteers. Here, engines arrive from two different departments and the firefighters show a wide range of dress representing the fact that they left their jobs or homes to join the engine and get to the fire. Turnout gear differs among them, and some are not wearing any gear at all.

## Who These Dedicated People Are

Firefighters are people from all walks of life who share a common bond—the longing to be there for other people. They are individuals who train diligently to learn their jobs and require great physical strength and endurance to perform their duties. They possess a passion for excitement and aren't afraid of adding some danger to their life. They also have the mental capacity to push past pain and emotions, enabling them to charge into a burning building because innocent civilians are counting on them to save lives and property just as previous generations of firefighters have done.

# A Firefighter's Call to Duty

**R**ick Kolomay is a lieutenant with the Schaumburg Fire Department in Illinois. As of this writing, he has been a career firefighter for 24 years. Preceding him in the fire service were his father, Sully, and his uncles, Richard (Rip) Kolomay and Mike Szewczyk. All three served the Chicago Fire Department. Sully was with Engine Company 98 and retired after 38 1/2 years. Rip was assigned to Engine Companies 14 and 89 and held citywide relief positions as an engineer and a lieutenant. He had a total of 38 years on the job.   Mike was with Hook and Ladder Company 19 and dedicated 29 years to the city.

Rick remembers visiting his father's firehouse in the summer of 1964 when he was only six years old. His dad had recently been promoted to engineer, designating him as a driver and pump operator for Engine 98. Rick did not realize that he was visiting the firehouse that day so he could ride on the engine for the first time. As the trio sat outside the station waiting for the bell to ring, his father and uncle became increasingly impatient with the quiet shift.

When the calm could no longer be tolerated by Rip, he placed a phone call to Rick's mom with very specific instructions. She was to call the fire department and report a rubbish fire at a particular location. The call would enable young Rick to get on the rig and respond with the engine for his maiden run. Soon after, the bell rang for what turned out to be an anticipated false alarm and it preceded several other authentic calls that required a response from Engine 98.

These ridealongs became much more frequent with Rick ringing the big bell on the way back to quarters. Since the firehouse had a second floor with sleeping quarters, the firemen had brass poles to slide down into the apparatus bay when the alarm sounded. Sully was concerned that Rick could inadvertently fall down one of the pole holes, so overnight visits meant Rick would sleep in the front seat of the engine under the eye of the firefighter on watch. When the alarm rang, the pillow and blanket were whisked away and Rick was in place and ready to go, always being careful to give his dad enough room to change gears on the manual transmission.

Years later at a small rubbish fire, Rick was allowed to hold the pipe on the attack line, a moment that he believes sealed his decision to pursue the fire service as a career. He loved to listen to the older guys and learn from them as he grew older and then tested for a position at a suburban Chicago department. He eventually joined the Schaumburg Fire Department, which was then under the command of Fire Chief Robert Sutherland. Chief Sutherland was an old-time firefighter who had retired after 17 years with the city of Chicago. Something that greatly impressed and interested Rick in the Schaumburg Fire Department was that Chief Sutherland ran this department with great respect for the rich traditions of the fire service until he passed away in 1990. Today, Rick works alongside Scott Sutherland, the ex-chief's son who has 28 years on the job.

Now Rick's teenage son Brandon, who responded on his first fire run at the age of seven, has decided to follow the family tradition and become the third generation Kolomay in the fire service. He joined a local fire department explorer post and has the benefit of being able to accompany his dad, a field fire instructor, during certain training sessions. Brandon visits with his father at the firehouse and receives verbal jabs from the other guys with the same regularity as a full-time brother.

Rick's nine-year-old daughter Noelle, who has learned special team skills from her father like rappelling, also has expressed a potential interest in joining the family business when she is older.

For Rick, little in the world can substitute for the pride and rich fire service traditions that pass through three generations.

LEFT: Schaumburg Fire Department Lieutenant Rick Kolomay and his father, retired engineer Sully Kolomay of the Chicago Fire Department (CFD) Engine Company 98, flank Rick's son, Brandon. Sully took Rick for his first ridealong at age six. Sully's brother and brother-in-law also retired after devoting many years to the Chicago Fire Department. Brandon wants to carry on the family tradition and become the third generation family member to enter the fire service. He started riding along when he was just seven.

BELOW: In 1966, young Rick got to visit the Chicago Fire Department training academy, which included the opportunity to investigate several rigs. He is pictured here sitting on the tailboard of Snorkel 4. *Photo courtesy of Rick Kolomay*

Firefighters also are individuals who don't want desk jobs; they want the ability to work indoors and outside through the course of their shift. These are people who must function without faltering in the hottest weather when they are on the brink of heat exhaustion, and on the coldest days when everything around them, including their clothing and gear, is covered with ice. Since emergencies occur at all times of the day and night, firefighters are expected to work through meals and without sleep if necessary. They are people who are capable of dropping everything at the sound of an alarm and channeling all of their energy, presence, and determination to meet any challenge that they are faced with.

Completely giving of themselves, firefighters give their all to the job, to their co-workers, and to the residents of the cities and communities that they serve. Most have even more to offer, assisting benevolent organizations by donating their time and through fundraising efforts. They collect toys for disadvantaged children at Christmastime and have raised funds for the Muscular Dystrophy Association (MDA) for almost 50 years.

The firefighter of today also is a member of a profession that is steeped with proud traditions, one of those being the decisions of multiple generations of families to join the ranks. It is not uncommon to have sons and daughters follow fathers, uncles, aunts, cousins, and mothers into the fire service.

The examples of a fire service family run deep. A recent trip to California brought me into contact with a female career firefighter for the University of California at Davis, whose husband is a career firefighter on the Sacramento City Fire Department. In suburban Chicago there is a retired battalion chief whose father-in-law was a firefighter and whose eldest son is both a career firefighter and a volunteer. And after the heroic efforts of the FDNY personnel on September 11,

2001, the battalion chief's youngest son decided to pursue the fire service as well contrary to his previous thoughts.

One firefighter who contributed to this book followed his father and two uncles into the fire service, and he expects his teenage son and possibly his younger daughter to follow as well. Another contributor is a deputy district chief with 23 years on the job whose father, a former fire commissioner, uncle and great uncle retired after dedicating a combined 102 years of service to the Chicago Fire Department. These examples are only a handful of fire service family relationships, which are common throughout the country and often are not broken by the loss of a loved one. In fact, many fire service families that have lost a loved one in the line of duty continue their dedication to the fire service as additional family members pursue the job with pride and resolve.

## What's the Lure?
### The Pay and Benefits

For many career firefighters, the pay is decent, but the tangible and intangible benefits are very good. Except in times of dire financial straits for municipal governments, job security for firefighters is excellent. Health and death benefits are strong, as well as pensions for retirement. Volunteer firefighters often can rely on their fire department affiliations for health care and pension benefits, as well as stipends, depending on the compensation their department offers.

Since many paid firefighters join the fire service at an early age, they can be fully vested while still in their prime, and some then take the opportunity to begin again with a different department that allows them to qualify for a second set of retirement benefits. Firefighters also work long shifts. These condensed work schedules generally provide time for second jobs, plenty of free

Larry Nelson, a veteran firefighter with FDNY Rescue 5 on Staten Island, serves as the driver of the rig for this tour. Because he is behind the wheel, he is more comfortable without his bunker coat as he drives to the scene of the fire.

time, and, in many cases, significant overtime. Depending on the area of the country and the particular fire department, a firefighter's schedule is most likely one of the following: Twenty-four hours on followed by 48 hours off, which is a 48-hour work week; 24 hours on followed by 24 hours off, which is a 42 hour week; two nine-hour day shifts followed by 48 hours off that precede two 15-hour night tours, which are then followed by three days off, for an average 40.5-hour week.

Firefighters join the fire service for many different reasons. First of all, as outlined above, the pay, benefits, and work schedule are enticing to some. Depending on the specific department, fire duty can be limited, which lowers the possibility of life-threatening danger. Then there are others who do not get into firefighting for the money or for the job's health care and retirement benefits. They love the job so much that they might even do it for no pay at all but rather for the sheer excitement and love of the fire service. These firefighters are motivated by the chance to save a life, to run into a burning building, or to render aid to someone who is dying. Somewhere in between the tangeble (pay and benefits) and the intangible (adrenaline rush), lies the lure for most firefighters.

### The Excitement

Truly there are few jobs capable of providing the thrill that occurs when the alarm rings for a working fire (an actual fire, as opposed to an automatic alarm or incidental small fire), a bad wreck, or other life-threatening disaster. To begin with, imagine rushing to the scene with emergency lights flashing, an old-fashioned Federal-Q mechanical siren wailing, and someone stomping on a real air horn while the driver blows through intersections, navigates through heavy traffic, and passes everyone else along the way. Listening en route to radio chatter giving reports of the incident and then pulling up to find mayhem, chaos, and people desperate for help can get anyone's adrenaline pumping. Then knowing that you have the training, the proper equipment, the expertise, and what it takes to march forward and tackle whatever comes your way is as fulfilling as anything in life.

Rushing into the burning building as everyone else is escaping, searching through the smoke and heat for the source of the fire or for victims, while relying on your "brothers" to assist you, provide backup, and enable you to succeed is what firefighting is all about. Charging into a fire is comparable to going into battle: The outcome is dependant on the soundness of the battle plan, the abilities and the willingness of the soldiers, and perhaps a mixture of common sense and good luck. Making a good stop, which refers to a quick knock down of the fire and stopping it from creating any further damage, is exhilarating because that means the battle was waged well. Saving the property you signed on to protect gives an added sense of triumph.

Risking personal injury and death, a firefighter's passion for helping others is satisfied only after giving everything they have. It doesn't get any better that that for firefighters. Additional pride stems from emerging from a burning building after having saved a prized pet and returning it to the family whose home has just gone up in flames. The family is devastated at the loss of or damage to their home but grateful for the safe return of a loved companion.

### The People
Over and over again, the majority of firefighters young and old from around the country, and specifically those who contributed to this book, have stated the same thing about the job's top benefit: The best part of the job is the people, period. Those that are in the fire service claim that you'll never find a better group of people to work with. The close-knit environment, the friendships, and the interdependency on one another in the fire service is incomparable to any other profession, especially when taking into consideration the ever present life-threatening aspect of the job.

Firefighters also enjoy the people they come into contact with while answering calls or doing other service for the community. These citizens show respect for the important job that firefighters do and make the firefighters feel appreciated for their efforts and sacrifices. This admiration means a lot to firefighters.

### What It Takes to Be a Firefighter
Movies, television shows, and books depict firefighters as rugged, heroic, strong, and dedicated, individuals with "the right stuff." All of this is true of course, but more importantly many traits of a firefighter come from the heart, such as feeling the need to serve and help other people whether they are friends or strangers. Firefighters also need to work well as part of a team, be outgoing, be self-disciplined, and have self-confidence. They also must be willing to go where most won't and do what many can't in order to save and protect the lives and properties of others—to run towards a tragic event or into a burning building when seemingly sane people are running the opposite direction. But most importantly, the four cornerstones of being a firefighter are the following: duty, dedication, honor, and courage.

Firefighting also requires great physical strength and endurance. Working on the scene of a fire, also called the fireground, includes wearing heavy bunker gear, boots, and a helmet while being able carrying an air pack and heavy tools. While loaded down like this, firefighters must be able to move quickly, climb steep ladders to the upper floors or roof, and crawl under the heat and smoke dragging a charged hose line.

# Thinking About Becoming a Firefighter

If you are considering a full-time career as a firefighter, most departments today will require a two- or four-year college degree. This requirement has changed in recent years from previous thinking that it was important to have a trade prior to entering the fire service. As important as a trade skill is to supplement fire service training, modern-day firefighters are constantly undergoing additional training to keep up with changes in the job. Whereas it used to be the case that homework ended when one left school, homework does not stop for a modern-day firefighter. They take college classes as well as specialized courses to boost their skills on a regular basis.

Logic, reasoning, computer skills, and writing skills are all necessary in order to rise through the ranks of the fire service today. Leadership and problem-solving capabilities also contribute to the success of a firefighter. So does the realization that the job entails real danger and the possibility of injury or death. Tasks that require tremendous strength, such as breaking down doors and pulling ceilings, make it necessary for a firefighter to be in top physical condition. This strength is augmented in today's fire service by the need to be able to perform skilled evaluations to test for life-threatening chemical and biological agents. This ability is superceded still by the required knowledge of how to handle a situation in which a responder or member of the public comes in contact with a deadly substance.

The expression on this firefighter's face offers a glimpse into the enjoyment and thrill of the job. Returning from the front lines carrying his ax, he is totally drenched from head to toe. His eyes are red from being subjected to smoke, but he wears a wide grin of exhilaration.

They may have to drag large amounts of hose up stairways and ladders, or carry unconscious or disoriented victims down ladders, then throw off their helmets and masks to render first aid to those victims.

If these tasks aren't already enough to demand an incredible degree of strength, firefighters need to summon every ounce of energy when the need arises to bail out of a dangerous environment. Some say that in order to be a firefighter, you can't be scared. Others say that if you're not scared, you may be foolish, reckless, and run the risk of endangering yourself or others unnecessarily. The truth lies somewhere in between. Indeed, bravery is required to enter a burning building. But many people that are not firefighters have performed this heroic task without ever intending to, including police officers, neighbors, family members, and random passersby. Driven by the inherent desire to help others, many from all walks of life summon the courage to help in such emergencies. These incidents are different from someone making a conscious choice to pursue this endeavor as a career or volunteer, though. Smart and responsible reactions to such emergency situations are fostered by the training and teamwork that are stressed in the fire service

Another trait that firefighters develop is the need to become hardened to life's tragedies, not unlike other professionals in medicine and law enforcement. Death, destruction, sorrow, misfortune, loss, tragedy, and dealing with the emotional pain of others are all circumstances that will be encountered. The ability to help strangers, to comfort others, and yet to remove oneself from each incident gives firefighters the strength to continue. Therefore, being unable to distance yourself from tragedies could be detrimental to a firefighter's mental and physical well being.

In the end, the job is not for everyone.

When the alarm rings and the pagers are activated for a volunteer fire company, firefighters respond from wherever they are, wearing their work or leisure clothing. They may all look alike with full bunker gear, but when they remove their coats it becomes obvious that they're not wearing matching uniforms. Two firefighters here confer on the scene of a residential fire in suburban Pittsburgh.

# CHAPTER 2
# Tools of the Trade

Firefighters need to be in top physical condition to perform their tasks optimally. Here, a firefighter assigned to a truck company begins to climb the aerial ladder to a roof. He is fully dressed in turnout gear and wearing his self-contained breathing apparatus (SCBA) while also carrying a life rope for searches over his right shoulder and irons in his left hand.

M odern-day firefighters receive a tremendous amount of technical training on a variety of personal equipment and firefighting tools, which enable them to perform their duties with speed, accuracy, and great skill. So knowing the tasks that are required for the job is just a portion of a firefighter's required learning. Common everyday tools and gear, plus some items that are unique to the fire service, are very much a part of the firefighter's life. These items include special clothing and uniforms to protect a firefighter's body from burns, hand tools, power tools, ladders, hoses, nozzles, and specialized vehicles to transport personnel and equipment.

### Clothing and Personal Protection Gear

Gone are the days of pure polyester, acrylic, and other synthetic uniforms. Research has determined that the flammability of this type of clothing can provide a potentially life-threatening danger to firefighters. Now cotton and other fabrics with flame-retardant materials are used for the shirts, pants, and sweatshirts that are worn while on duty.

On-scene, a firefighter wears turnout gear. Most commonly, this gear includes a short or three-quarter length bunker coat, matching pants that are fashioned to come up underneath the bottom of the coat, and either leather or rubber boots that extend to the mid calf. The boots fit inside of the bunker pants, allowing

Here is another image from the late 1970s of an engine officer on-scene in Chicago. He chose not to pull up his boots and has no protection around his neck or chest as is provided today by the protective hoods and high coat collars. In those days, firefighters rarely utilized SCBA, as was not the tradition. As a matter of fact, in many fire departments, peer pressure was such that using a mask inside a building was seen as a sign of weakness.

This image from a 4-11 alarm fire on Chicago's north side in 1979 shows an officer listening to a chief in front of the fire building. The Chicago Fire Department still utilizes three-quarter rubber hip boots and long coats as seen here. The officer on the left chose not to pull his boots up and as a result has pants that are soaking wet. He is wearing an older-style plastic helmet while the chief has a more traditional leather helmet. While the officer is not wearing any gloves, the chief took advantage of a pair of thin cotton gloves that were provided by the Salvation Army.

the firefighter to get into them before using suspenders (red or otherwise) to pull the pants up. But some departments still utilize an older-style gear. This gear includes a longer coat, which often has a rubber exterior coating and is used in conjunction with rubber hip boots. These boots fold down for easy access and can be pulled up to the inner thigh to keep the firefighter dry. Turnout coats used to be rubber or canvas, the latter of which took quite awhile to dry after getting wet at a fire. The rubber and canvas were replaced with newer materials such as Basofil, Nomex, Kevlar, Fire-Dex and PBI, designed to provide significantly better protection from heat and fire. The new pants offer greater protection than the older hip boots did because they protect firefighters' legs, hips, and thighs when crawling through burning buildings.

Leather, plastic, fiberglass, and rubber-coated helmets protect a firefighter's head, but many firefighters prefer the leather helmets because wearing them represents a longstanding tradition in the fire service. Although leather helmets are heavy, they don't provide as much shock protection as high-strength plastic, and are considerably more costly. To overcome this preference, several helmet builders have fashioned the plastic and fiberglass helmets to closely resemble the leather design and offer leather-covered helmets with a much stronger shell underneath.

All helmets show signs of wear from heat and smoke residue and damage. A well-worn helmet is the sign of a firefighter who has seen plenty of action. Most helmets have some sort of decorative front piece, which is made of leather, plastic, or simple vinyl decals. These front pieces represent the name of the fire department and often the particular company assignment of the firefighter. They are susceptible to heat and smoke damage, which add to the personalization of the helmet.

Contrasting the earlier fire scenes shown on previous pages, this modern image shows a suburban firefighter with full bunker gear consisting of a turnout coat and pants. The yellow device on his SCBA harness is a personal alert safety system (PASS) and his Nomex hood is bunched around his neck so that he can keep cool when he's not fighting the fire. He also has heavy work gloves to protect his hands.

In the past, part of the tradition of wearing a leather helmet was to shape its rear brim, which extends behind the firefighter's head. Molding the brims to curl up was the sign of a squad member in some departments, while a downward curl meant the firefighter was assigned to an engine. Keeping the brim flat was the sign of a truckie. Curling the brim upward kept hot embers and debris from falling down and burning the firefighter's neck when pulling ceilings. The downward curl, while sometimes fashioned just for looks, provided a channel for the water to run down the back of a firefighter's coat so that it would not puddle and rain down unexpectedly. This style worked for engine company members because they were tasked with hitting the fire with water.

A modern hood made of high-tech flame-resistant materials, such as Carbon Shield, Nomex, and PBI, provides a defense against heat and fire for the back of the head, ears, the face around an air mask, plus neck areas that were previously exposed. The use of hoods has significantly reduced the number of burns in these areas. The last bit of necessary clothing that firefighters wear is a good pair of work gloves made from Fire-Dex, Nomex, or Kevlar. These materials shield both heat and water, enabling firefighters good use of their hands while working on-scene.

In addition to the clothing that is worn for protection in a fire, several other crucial elements are a part of each firefighter's personal gear. The first is the self-contained breathing apparatus (SCBA). This piece of equipment consists of a mask, or face piece, with a breathing tube that attaches to an air cylinder in a harness, which is worn on the firefighter's back. The cylinders are made of a fiberglass composite to reduce the weight, whereas older designs were metal and as such were considerably heavier. The air pack harness has been improved for better weight distribution too and made by some manufacturers

The firefighters pictured here show that different types and colors of gear, including the varying placement or styles of the reflective stripes on their clothing, can serve to differentiate each fire department. Helmet designs can also be an indicator of a firefighter's company. This company, with tools in hand, is returning to the rig after being released by command.

Two firefighters fully dressed with turnout gear, SCBA, gloves, and fire resistant hoods take a breather for some fluid replenishment at the scene of a house fire. Their wet and dirty bunker pants indicate that they have spent time crawling around the fire floor under the heat and smoke of the fire before being relieved.

to fit the contour form of the back. The newer air cylinders can hold more air than the older designs could, and therefore, firefighters are able to work longer. The duration of any air cylinder depends on the breathing characteristics of the person wearing it, but the tanks are rated to supply breathing air for anywhere between 30 and 60 minutes, depending on the design.

Over the years, the mask has been improved for safety, allowing for increased visibility and enhanced communication capabilities. Some masks utilize integrated microphones that eliminate the need for a firefighter to use one hand to hold onto a radio. Masks also can be customized with corrective lenses to match a firefighter's vision deficiencies. A big advantage in newer designs is that they increase visibility by reducing the amount of fogging that occurs as a result

of a firefighter exhaling in the mask. This effect is achieved with a nose cone that isolates the exhaled breath from the rest of the mask's vision field. Although most SCBAs are shared, several years ago fire departments began assigning masks to each firefighter.

Another safety measure incorporated into the SCBA is a provision for buddy breathing, whereby a trapped firefighter who is running out of air can receive fresh air by connecting to another's SCBA, or from a spare air bottle that is brought in to help the downed firefighter. This allows the rescuing firefighter from having to go without air. In the past, a firefighter would remove his mask, hold his breath, and allow the other firefighter to take a breath from the same mask before switching back and forth several times. To ensure the safe use and manufacture

These firefighters work in San Francisco. The four on the left are assigned to Ladder 5 and the officer on the right is with Engine 21. The helmets of the truck crew feature red- and white-painted panels, which provide distinction on the scene. Two members of the truck company have lights affixed to their helmets keeping their hands free for other tools. The white strips of material on their turnout coats are reflective to make them more visible at night, providing an added margin of personal safety.

of the SCBA the NFPA governs all aspects of the apparatus and is constantly reviewing and updating regulations pertaining to the repair, replacement, and allowable lifespan of this equipment.

The next important tool that is part of the personal gear for each firefighter is a personal alert safety system (PASS). This alarm used to be a separate piece of equipment that was attached to the front of the SCBA harness and was turned on separately from the SCBA's air flow. Current models are integrated into the harness and operate with the air pack. They also can be built into the SCBA gauge. Some PASS devices now include a locater so that someone in the command post knows where all of the firefighters are when they have their air packs turned on. The PASS emits a piercing sound and sometimes a visual alarm when it detects no movement for a

The driver of an engine is also the pump operator. Here, he has positioned Engine 13 a block away from the fire and is supplying two large diameter lines, which are either being used to augment another engine or are split into smaller attack lines closer to the fire. This unusual-looking compact rig has been designed with an electronic pump panel at the rear of the unit. Placement on the right side of the vehicle would normally allow the operator to be on the curb side of the street, away from traffic. Additionally, all of the discharges and intakes are located at the rear of this rig, directly under the hose bed.

Firefighters in San Francisco wear turnout coats and their uniform pants with waterproof boots. Here, two firefighters standing by at a commercial fire alarm talk as they await instructions from the chief. Firefighters have assignments based on their riding positions on the rig. Both are equipped with SCBA and different configurations of fire hose to bring into the building in the event of a fire.

predetermined period of time, which could be anywhere from 30 seconds to several minutes. These alarms are meant to alert other firefighters to the location of a fallen, trapped, incapacitated, or unconscious firefighter.

### Personal Tools

Each firefighter is responsible for certain hand tools, some of which are assigned individually. These may include an ax and a haligan tool or pry bar, which together are referred to as the irons (a term that stems from the original material that they were made of). The haligan bar is a uniquely designed tool that has a claw at one tip for lifting and prying and on the other end has a flat wedge for door breaching and a pointed tip for pulling or puncturing. This tool, which has a shaft that is usually heavily taped so that it can be easily gripped, is often used in conjunction with an ax. A firefighter uses the ax like a hammer to pound the haligan and put more force into an attempt to pry something open. Another common tool used with the irons is a flathead or pick head ax, which can break, shatter, and tear down walls, signs, or furniture and execute other chores. (Still wondering about the lure to this job?)

The next vital tool is the common flashlight, which every firefighter must have. Some carry a large light on a leather spanner's or truckman's belt; others sling the light on a strap over their neck and shoulder. Some just grab a handheld light from the vehicle that they ride on and carry it in their hand, while others mount a smaller light on their helmet allowing them free use of both hands. Many seasoned firefighters also add a couple of simple wooden door wedges to the tools that they carry. The wedges are used to prop doors open for easy access and escape or egress, while at the same time allowing for the unencumbered placement of hose lines and movement of personnel. The wedge is tucked inside an elastic band that wraps around the helmet. The seasoned firefighter will supplement the items carried based on personal experience and may also add a screwdriver, a knife, a wrench, a pliers, a roll of tape, or any one of a number of other common household items.

A crucial tool that many firefighters go without due to financial constraints is a portable radio. At times, this is a life-saving device. But it is more often just an incredibly useful tool to assist with finding the location of personnel and for relaying vital information to the chief who then makes informed decisions regarding strategies for extinguishing the fire. While some fire departments are able to outfit each firefighter with a portable radio, others simply assign one radio per company of four to five people. Another tool many fire departments go without because of its expense is a thermal imaging unit. The unit, which uses infrared technology, helps firefighters locate unconscious victims and dangerous hot spots.

## Vehicles and Equipment

Although very important, the tools carried by the firefighter do not take into account the basic necessities of firefighting, most commonly the hose, ladders, and pike poles. This equipment is assigned to and stored on vehicles, most commonly referred to as the rigs. Rig types include pumpers, aerials, rescue units, and medic units.

### Pumpers

A pumper, also known as an engine, has a fire pump and carries water, several types of hose, nozzles, and the appropriate fittings to tap a fire hydrant. The official term for an engine is a triple-combination apparatus. This name infers that the unit has three distinct characteristics: a pump, water, and hose. SCBA, ground ladders, and other assorted tools are also carried on the engine. The personnel assigned to the engine are referred to as the engine company. This group of firefighters can range from an understaffed crew of two to a full crew of six, including a driver and a company officer who is in charge.

The officer shares the front-forward facing seats with the driver and handles radio communications. The firefighters ride in the back of the cab, either facing forward or backward depending on the design of the rig's cab. Before all personnel were required by the NFPA to be seated with safety restraints, firefighters were commonly

When a fire gets the better of a structure, the fire department goes on the defensive and withdraws companies from operating inside the building and pulls everyone back to a safe distance that is clear of a potential collapse zone. These firefighters are directing their stream in through a second-floor window of an apartment complex where the fire has gotten out of control and burned through the roof. When this defensive tactic is used on all sides of the building and from elevated master streams, it is commonly referred to as a "surround and drown" operation.

Firefighters in San Clemente, California, were allowed to wear short pants as part of their work uniforms in the early 1980s. Many departments throughout the country have since adopted this uniform during the hot summer months including the FDNY. San Clemente ran with yellow apparatus, including this 1980 Crown Firecoach pumper.

seen standing in the rear jump seat area of the cab, or riding on the rear step of the rig and hanging on to a bar so they wouldn't fall off.

Using charged hoses to attack fires with water is the primary responsibility of the firefighters assigned to the engine. The driver, referred to on the East Coast as the chauffeur, positions the rig to secure a continuous water supply from a hydrant, which supplements the water that is stored on the rig. At the same time, firefighters pull hoses from the rig before advancing on the fire in an aggressive attempt to extinguish it, prevent further damage to property, and stop the threat to others' safety.

One popular type of nozzle used at the end of a hose is called a smooth-bore tip, which is sometimes referred to as a "pipe" since it is a brass pipe that narrows slightly from the diameter of the hose to the open end of the nozzle. Another type of tip is a fog nozzle which is adjustable to allow a straight stream or fog pattern similar to what is commonly used on a garden hose.

A firefighter from Chicago Engine Company 62 grabs a load of 1 3/4-inch attack line off the rear of the engine. He'll take the attack line to the rear of a bungalow where the back porch is engulfed in flames. After securing a hydrant, the engineer will uncouple the hose from the bed and connect to a discharge port on the back of the rig so that he can supply water to the line when the firefighters request it by radio.

From the first day on the job, candidates are instilled with the notion that they "never give up the pipe" when directing the attack line as this is a traditional position of honor. However, when a more aggressive company approaches the scene wanting to advance the attack, the first company on the scene might give up the nozzle if it is unable to advance any further. Some old timers tell stories of fistfights exchanged between firefighters dueling over who would gain control over the pipe at a fire scene. These kinds of skirmishes were abundant in the 1800s when competing fire companies would arrive at a fire and fight to get first water on the job, often resulting in losing the firefight because of a fistfight.

One Chicago chief tells a story of being at a fire in a one-story commercial building on the city's south side some years ago. After explaining that Chicago Fire Department protocol prohibits hose lines from going into or coming out of windows, he said that he witnessed an attack line that went into the rear door of the building, out a nearby window, and then went back into the building through the door. After getting over his initial confusion, he sought out the company officer to determine just what the heck was going on. Before he finished chewing out the officer for trying to gift wrap the building, a probationary firefighter tried to intervene but was immediately shut down.

Instead of settling the matter right there, the chief and company officer decided to continue the attack at hand and agreed to discuss the situation at a post-fire debriefing. Later, the other firefighters explained to the chief that the probationary firefighter, or probie, had the pipe and that

This winter house fire has required the use of many tools and other items off the pumper squad (an engine with more than normal storage space) positioned in front. The pump operator is responsible for all of the items assigned to the rig in addition to monitoring the pump to maintain the required water pressure for the attack lines being used. The fire is not close to being out, and already this engine has supplied hose, ladders, a haligan bar, spare SCBA bottles, and a long pike pole. Since the pump operator will not be involved in the firefight, he can decide whether to suit up in bunker gear.

One method of donning SCBA is by slipping each arm through the appropriate strap when the unit is in a seat bracket inside the truck's cab. Another method, demonstrated here by firefighters in Oshkosh, Wisconsin, is by grabbing the air pack and hoisting it overhead while slipping both arms through the harness straps at the same time. Many fire departments sew the names of each firefighter on the back of their turnout coats. The low placement of names on these coats allows them to be visible even when the firefighters are wearing their SCBAs. The truck in this image is an example of a quint with a rear-mounted telescoping aerial ladder. The large section with gauges and levers is the pump panel. Proof of an onboard water tank is not available visually, but this rig has one.

the others who were slightly behind him were immersed in a dense smoke with no visibility. As the probie ran out of air, he remembered the rule about never giving up the pipe, so he determined that the proper move was to keep the pipe in hand and to bail out the nearest window so that he could change out his air bottle. As it turned out, the window was about six feet off the ground. As the company officer and other firefighters on the line noticed the nozzle man moving forward, they did not have enough time to stop him from going out the window. Since they no longer had the protection of the line, the rest of the company bailed out.

Upon regrouping, the company members determined that they would not be able to get back in through the same window, so they advanced the line again through the open door. Since the fire service requires the ability to improvise to overcome any obstacles, the chief found it difficult to come down hard on the rookie firefighter for reacting the best way he could to something that he'd been taught. The chief settled for qualifying the rule by saying that it's OK to share the pipe within your own company, but not OK to give it to another company.

On each shift, every firefighter has a specific riding position on a rig and assignments relating

Here is another "surround and drown" operation where the volume of water being applied to the fire is so great that the street is flooding. Because not much more can be done to drown the flames, these two firefighters stand back and wait for a new assignment. They are from different fire departments as exhibited by the different bunker gear that they are wearing.

After ventilating the third-floor windows with a long pike pole from the safety of the second-floor roof landing, truck company members descend a 35-foot ladder. Each firefighter is wearing full bunker gear, a SCBA, and heavy gloves for their protection.

to the type of emergencies they are responding to. For example, a firefighter riding in the back of an engine to a reported fire may be responsible for grabbing a pump can and an ax when pulling up and seeing no visible fire. If a fire is visible, this firefighter's responsibility will be to pull an attack line and proceed to the fire. While the driver finds a fire hydrant for a continuous water supply, the officer sizes up the scene to determine the extent of the fire. An automobile accident might require the firefighter to grab a first aid kit if they have medical training, a pry bar if the door needs to be popped open, or a small trash line in the event of fluid leaks or the threat of a fire, while the driver prepares the pump in the event that they will use the water. Night incidents will require the driver to utilize rig-mounted lighting to illuminate the area for added safety. Because any piece of equipment could be needed at any time, each company member must know the complete layout of the vehicle and the proper placement of each item.

### Aerial Apparatus

The aerial truck, commonly just called a truck, has a master aerial device capable of extending from roughly 50 feet to lengths in excess of 100 feet, depending on the style and type of unit. These can be telescoping ladders, which are on the majority of trucks that are in service, or articulating devices that sometimes have a platform at the end. Another aerial device, which is one of the most popular ones being ordered now, combines a ladder with a platform at the end and is called a platform aerial, tower ladder, or ladder tower. Design elements of each device offer either a rear mounting of the ladder base, where the ladder tip rests over the cab of the truck, or a midship-mounted unit, where the ladder or platform tip hangs past the rear of the vehicle. A third type of aerial, which is called a

Rehabilitation, or rehab, is an important aspect of safety for firefighters at the scene of a working fire. Here, six suburban firefighters are in rehab at the scene of an extra alarm fire on a hot summer day. They are drinking water to replace fluids that were lost through sweat and taking advantage of wet towels to help cool off. It is not unusual on hot and humid days for fires to escalate in terms of the required manpower needed in an effort to offset a reduction in the amount of time that firefighters can function before they need to be replaced with fresh crews.

tractor-drawn or tillered aerial, has a tractor that pulls the aerial device on a trailer, at the end of which is a cab for one firefighter who steers the rear axle.

By mandate, the aerial carries a greater number of ground ladders than the pumper, as well as more loose tools. Often a generator is on a truck, plus specialized tools that are used when responding to vehicle wrecks and ropes that are used in many types of rescue operations. Some trucks are being designed now so that they provide the same functions as an engine. In this case, the truck is called a quint, which stands for quintessential fire apparatus. This truck is a specialized unit with five distinct characteristics: the first three are the same as the triple combination pumper (a pump, a water tank, and several types of hose), a full complement of ground ladders, and a master arial device which is permanently affixed.

The aerial or truck company is tasked with search and rescue operations as well as forcible entry and ventilation. The truck company, or truckies, tell stories about anxious residents or neighbors waiting outside a burning building, frantically telling them of others trapped inside. Most often the firefighters can tell by the tone in the people's voices, their emotions, and their gestures that they're telling the truth, at which point the truck company will make every attempt to make entry and search for the victims. However, some big city veterans recall incidents where those waiting outside were putting on a great show to lead the firefighters on, trying to trick them just to see them go in and get dirty.

Truckies utilize different tools that are not as familiar to the average person in comparison to the attack hose of an engine. Truckies carry the irons, the pike pole, chain saws, circular saws, and a sledgehammer. A pike pole is a wooden or fiberglass pole of varying lengths with a steel hook on one end. The hook is used to poke through walls or ceilings, allowing the firefighter to pull the drywall or other building material away from the studs. Pulling down this material lets the firefighter check for the extension or spread of a fire.

The truck company also breaks windows and cuts holes in the roof to ventilate the structure. The importance of ventilation is tantamount to a successful attack. Ventilating a structure allows for the intentional escape of heat, noxious gases, and smoke, all of which hamper the efforts of the engine company by making the interior conditions

A heavy rescue squad is a giant toolbox on wheels, carrying as much equipment and supplies as the fire department deems necessary to handle a multitude of emergencies. This is a Saulsbury heavy rescue unit from Marcellus, New York, showing hydraulic tools, saws, cribbing, air bags, power tools, a telescoping light tower, and many other items. This photo only shows one side of the vehicle. The other side is full of equipment and tools as well. Realizing that this is but one side of the vehicle, it is easy to imagine how much additional equipment is on the other side, in the upper compartments, and in the rear compartments that are built into the stairs.

extremely difficult to endure. Establishing good ventilation also reduces the likelihood of backdrafts which occur when a smoldering fire that is deprived of oxygen is fueled with a fresh supply

This cold winter fire in a suburb of Chicago in 1982 exemplifies the dedication of volunteer, paid-on-call, and off-duty personnel coming to the aide of a neighbor. Two of the responding firefighters went directly to the scene so they could render assistance instead of taking the additional time to get their gear from the firehouse. The unmatching fire coats shown also suggest that multiple departments were called to the scene.

After having a picture taken of their newly painted rig, the officer and firefighters assigned to FDNY Engine 4 in Manhattan posed for an informal group shot. Their 1981 Mack apparatus was representative of most FDNY rigs in the 1980s with fully enclosed seating for all of the personnel. It was not until the 1990s that the NFPA adopted regulations recommending that all fire departments provide fully enclosed cabs for the safety of firefighters, eliminating the ability to stand on the rear step or in the jump seat area. But the early use of fully enclosed apparatus by the FDNY stemmed from a need to protect firefighters from harm during periods of civil unrest.

of oxygen and explosively increases in size. If a fire burns through the roof of a structure, it has vented itself.

A firefighter riding on an aerial truck would get off the rig at a fire call carrying irons, a pike pole, or, if a person is needed on the roof, a power saw. Some departments do not require truck members that go to the roof to wear SCBA, which might be cumbersome. These departments feel that because the firefighters are outside, they

The truck company from Hook & Ladder No. 3 in Chicago posed here with the company's new 135-foot, E-ONE ladder in the spring of 1985. This unit was one of the first in the country to put a 135-foot ladder—the tallest ladder built in America—into service. The denim-looking uniforms were made of fire-resistant material in an effort to provide added protection, replacing the flammable polyester uniforms that preceded them.

will likely have enough air to breathe. In this situation, truckies are without their integrated PASS devices, so they need to have a stand-alone PASS device on their spanner's or truckman's belt, which may also hold a flashlight and an ax. Since the PASS alarm can activate after as little as 30 seconds of inactivity, some of the older veterans use them as a means of locating the duckers—the firefighters who aren't working.

Structure fires, although seemingly the mainstay of firefighters' emergency responses, are but a portion of their daily duties and calls. Very often they are called to the scene of motor vehicle accidents. These can range from the simple fender benders to terrible wrecks with trapped people who require medical attention and need to be removed or extricated from the vehicles. Similar to the arrival of an engine company at a car wreck, the truck company uses different tools for these responses than it would when responding to a fire.

### Rescue Unit or Squad

In addition to the pumper and aerial, fire departments often utilize rescue units or squads, which are big toolboxes on wheels. The squads carry more specialized tools and equipment than an engine or truck does. The rescue squads can range from a small utility body mounted on a three-quarter ton pickup truck chassis to an intricately designed custom-built truck on a commercial or custom fire truck chassis. The units also can be specially designed tractor-trailer combination units.

A blanket is used to protect the patient who is trapped in this overturned sport utility vehicle (SUV) from stray debris as a firefighter uses a hydraulic cutter to remove the door. The multitude of colored hoses on the ground provides a means for the fire department to differentiate between the different tools that company members have brought out to use. Wood cribbing is visible supporting the front of the vehicle, as is an inflated air bag that was inserted to lift the SUV off the street. A deflated air bag, the black rubber square shaped item with a large yellow "X," is in the foreground under the pile of cords.

Fitchburg, Wisconsin, firefighters use an assortment of tools to extricate an accident victim from a car. They have already removed the driver's door and are creating additional room to get access to the driver who is being protected with a tarp to prevent further injury. The victim is never without a firefighter alongside in the vehicle for comfort and assistance.

This is an example of a fire and EMS response from a volunteer fire department on Long Island. Two firefighter/paramedics responded with the ambulance, while several others went directly to the scene in their own vehicles from their jobs or home. Although one firefighter chose to don a safety vest, the others have nothing but their pagers and expertise to distinguish them from the bystanders. The ambulance that is on-scene is an example of a modern modular-type unit.

The rescue squad company's principle tool for extricating trapped victims of motor vehicle accidents is commonly known as the Jaws of Life. This is one part of a set of gas- or air-powered hydraulic tools that can cut, pry or spread apart a vehicle. Some require two firefighters to operate them, while others only require one. Although vehicle wrecks are the most common use for these tools, they can be used in any type of rescue where a victim is somehow trapped.

Another specialty tool used by rescue squad companies is an air bag, which is a flat square item made of neoprene rubber and Kevlar with steel fibers. The air bag can be inflated after being placed underneath a heavy object or between two objects that need to be separated. A rescue squad also will carry several types of saws, pry bars, and hand tools that can be used for breaking and pulling the windshield out of a vehicle, or cutting the seatbelts that cannot be released as designed.

Upon arrival at an accident scene or other rescue incident, the rescue squad company will evaluate the situation based on reports via the radio, a face-to-face meeting with other firefighters already on the scene, or by a visual examination of the accident. Most often, the rescue company uses tools similar to those that the truck company uses, including the irons, pike poles, and saws. Depending on when the rescue squad arrives on the scene, their assignment can range from search and rescue to ventilation or forcible entry but at least one firefighter grabs irons and basic tools in the event that the task is a simple one.

### Medic Units

Although an ambulance, or medic unit, is the most common type of vehicle used by EMS personnel, many conventional engines and trucks carry some medical equipment on board along with first responders, EMTs or even paramedics. Engines that are equipped with ALS equipment have all of the basic functions of an ambulance, including the presence of narcotics and telemetry equipment, but the vehicles can't transport patients. If the fire engine arrives on scene first, firefighters go to work stabilizing the patient until an ambulance arrives to carry the patient to the hospital.

When arriving at the scene, EMS personnel grab bandages, diagnostic tools, and splints as they head to attend to the victims. Drugs and telemetry equipment are also brought out if the emergency vehicles are ALS-equipped and emergency workers suspect that the scene includes those who are severely injured.

The addition of ALS and basic life support (BLS) functions directly relates to the increasing size of many ambulances. Ambulances used to

Buffalo Grove, Illinois, police, fire, and EMS crews are shown on the scene of a motor vehicle accident. As firefighter/paramedics assigned to the ambulance tend to the patient, firefighters from the engine and truck approach to see what assistance they can offer. They will inspect the vehicles for unsafe conditions and monitor any fluid leaks on the street.

be standard station wagons, which later progressed into larger wagons before maturing into vans by the early 1970s. When paramedics began administering BLS and ALS treatment, ambulances had to be larger so that they could accommodate both paramedics and EMTs who needed to move around in the unit. These larger modular units also offered more storage space for equipment and supplies.

# CHAPTER 3
# The Brotherhood

After the fire is out, firefighters like to relax a little. A smile, a cigar, and a joke can go a long way to overcome the stress, fear, or the adrenaline rush that comes from charging into a burning building and making a great save. That's why friendship and camaraderie are important aspects of the job.

The brotherhood is apparent here between this lieutenant and firefighter who were assigned to FDNY Rescue Company 4 from Queens in 1984. Even then, the FDNY was progressive with its use of multiple portable radios per company.

### It Begins with the Cup of Coffee

In all arenas of society, coffee is considered an icebreaker, a medium for conversation, and a means to make someone comfortable. In the fire service, a cup of coffee signifies even more. Throughout time, you could enter any active firehouse in the world and be offered a cup of coffee. It's a friendly gesture that represents far more than just a warm liquid beverage. It is part of the culture, the camaraderie that prevails. It speaks volumes about acceptance, warmth, being welcome, and most importantly, about the people. You will find this to be the rule everywhere that the true culture of the fire service prevails.

### In Quarters

Firefighting is truly a brotherhood. While many female firefighters have joined the fire service, the term that describes how tight-knit firefighters are remains the same. The concept goes beyond male and female or the blood relatives who are represented in the ranks. It encompasses every member of this second family and reflects the working environment that makes the fire service so special.

First of all, the brotherhood is fostered because of the lifestyle firefighters lead. Living together in a house creates a family-like environment. With firehouses having the same basic

Bunker gear for four firefighters stands ready for the next alarm. The leather boots protrude from the bunker pants for quick entry before pulling up on the suspenders. Coats are ready with radios, gloves, and at least one protective hood alongside a well-worn leather helmet. The fourth set of pants that is missing is most likely being worn around the station by a firefighter.

Teamwork is invaluable on the fireground. Here, Chicago firefighters work together to get two master streams into action at a 2-11 alarm fire on the city's north side. While firefighters work to lay a large diameter supply line so tower ladder 21 can go to work, another firefighter stands ready atop the engine to direct the deluge gun on the fire once the engine's supply line is charged.

features and amenities as residential homes, although varying in size and structure in relation to their surrounding communities, there are many of the same chores that must be performed: cleaning, shopping, making repairs, cooking, doing laundry, making the beds, and, of course, taking out the garbage. The chores are not all glamorous at times but are part of the job. Each person pitches in and works together.

Cooking can be communal or the task of an assigned individual. Most often, the kitchen features industrial appliances and storage areas that can accommodate large quantities of food. Many fire stations have three or four separate pantries and refrigerators to isolate supplies that are purchased by each shift. Every firefighter is asked to contribute a certain amount of money per shift to cover the cost of food as outlined by the day's menu. Often times, visitors or firefighters who

have been assigned from other stations to work a shift are not allowed to chip in to pay for the meal. The firefighters on duty may do the shopping together as a group or send the cook out alone if this does not disrupt the full complement of manpower needed to adequately respond when emergencies occur. Members of the Chicago Fire Department even have a specific provision in their contract that gives the cook one hour to shop.

Firehouse cooking has long been a popular subject and a sense of pride for numerous chefs. Some firefighters even boast, in private of course, that they eat better at the firehouse than at home with their spouses. A number of books have been written about firehouse cooking with favorite recipes and stories. Departments rich with tradition may have certain kitchen-related customs. For example, some departments do not recognize rank in the kitchen where the cook is king. If a complaint about the meal is made, the cook may turn the critic's plate upside down, signifying that food will not be offered. Then there's the treatment of the probies. Once assigned to a house, tradition in many departments dictates that the probies or rookies are the last in line to eat and the first ones up to do the dishes. This ritual can last through the formal probationary period or may continue until a newer candidate enters the house. With or without these traditions, dinnertime is important at the fire station, just as it is with other close families. Eating together gives firefighters time to talk and catch up on outside interests and news about their families.

While on-scene, the dirty faces point out the guys who went to work fighting the flames. However, there's always time to go back to quarters and wash up after the flames have been knocked down, it's time to slow down and chat with friends who might be assigned to another company. At fire scenes or training may be the only time that members of different companies get the chance to see each other and share a story or catch up on each other's lives.

Around the dinner table as well as throughout the house, the atmosphere and attitudes shown to other firefighters can differ drastically between departments that have differing degrees of "old school" tradition. To the outside observer, some of these interactions can be viewed as vulgar, rude, sarcastic, or perhaps antagonistic. Some choose to ridicule this behavior as archaic

Regardless of what is going on inside the firehouse, whether it involves chores, eating, studying, relaxing, or sleeping, firefighters must be ready to jump into the rig quickly when the bell rings to get on the road.

and outdated, portraying these firefighters in a negative light. But for many firefighters, such quips are part of the camaraderie and "all in good fun" environment that helps to unify the company as a family. Once the bell sounds, however, everyone's all business. But until that happens, this behavior is one way firefighters relieve stress and cope with a job that is extremely demanding.

When firefighters are not responding to a call, they have to ensure that the living quarters and the apparatus bays of the fire station are well maintained. All the house chores revolve around the time that is spent training and can't interfere with being on-call and ready to respond when the alarm sounds. Union departments have specific work rules about the amount of personal time that must be provided per shift, as well as time set aside for house chores. This work is not exclusive to career fire departments, as every fire station requires maintenance for its building, contents, equipment, and apparatus.

Each shift begins with checking personal equipment, including air packs and turnout gear. All of the equipment on the vehicles needs to be gone over, which includes starting all power tools and generators. Even though the previous shift did the same checks, firefighters who have just started their shift need to know that everything is in good working order instead of making assumptions with equipment that may be required to save someone's life. Although every time that equipment is used is not necessarily an emergency, seconds count when a life is at stake. Medical kits and tool kits are inspected as well as battery-operated items to ensure that they are operating correctly.

The vehicle drivers, chauffeurs, engineers, or pump operators are responsible for checking mechanical fluid levels, fuel, and the water tank on rigs that carry water. Each vehicle has an equipment inventory that is verified in the event that something was lost, stolen, or removed from the rig during the previous shift. Only after everything is in place and ready for the alarm to ring can the firefighters move on to the next task.

There's an old adage in the fire service stating that "The perfect house consists of one meeter, one greeter, one cook, one auto mechanic, and three dynamic firefighters." This statement means that each firehouse should have three great firefighters who may or may not have people skills, someone who knows how to cook for a crowd, someone who can work on the cars, and two firefighters who can make visitors feel at home when they stop by.

## The Culture

In many areas, tradition is the very fabric of the fire service. Part of this tradition is a culture of behavior and attitude that includes watching out for and helping one another on and off the job. Unfortunately, in many fire departments, this attitude has changed or disappeared. The old timers used to take the younger firefighters under their wing to teach and mentor them, taking the time to pass along information that was learned and experienced over 10, 15 or 20-plus years on the job. This mentoring relationship was in addition to whatever official training occurred for the new recruits.

But today, many fire departments rely heavily on the formal training, including books, videos, and PowerPoint presentations, as a means for all learning. This shift toward formal training is one reason why many of the most seasoned firefighters on the job get involved in training; they want to be in a position where they can bolster the official instruction with their seasoned skills and experiences to provide invaluable, practical lessons for others. For those seasoned veterans, there is no greater satisfaction than being able to offer newer firefighters information that may

Ready for a break, an engine company is preparing to rest after knocking down a residential house fire. They'll stay together as a crew outside as they did while working inside the structure. With helmets off, they'll remove their air packs and coats so they can cool down while others relieve them. Before they remove their SCBAs, they shut down the tanks using the valve at the base of the unit.

allow them to perform the job better and ensure the safety of the entire company.

This mentoring approach includes older veterans taking newer firefighters aside after they have been scared or involved in a particularly hairy event and talking to them. Oftentimes, the younger firefighters feel that their inexperience contributed to errors or problems that occurred during the call. But the veteran firefighters comfort them and explain that everything doesn't always go according to plan on the scene. The newer firefighters may have made mistakes, but often they have not, so the veterans must

stress being both aggressive and careful on the next call. Oftentimes the barn boss, the most senior firefighter in the house, takes on some of the responsibility of teaching and helping the younger firefighters adjust to their new roles in the department.

While the fading of some fire service traditions—such as veterans mentoring new recruits—is disappointing, other fire service traditions that have gone by the wayside have improved firefighter safety and opened the fire service to everyone. Mandating that firefighters be seated while the apparatus is in motion and incorporating

This classic image represents the fire service of the 1960s through the late 1980s before several factors combined to regulate fireground activity. Several guidelines were established by the National Fire Protection Association (NFPA) governing safety and personal protection of firefighters including the use of SCBA, fire resistant hoods, and the type of turnout gear that firefighters were permitted to wear. These Chicago firefighters from Engine Company 55 exhibit the old school without SCBA, with open collars, open coats, and rubber hip boots that leave their upper leg and hip areas unprotected as they train this attack line into the door of a commercial establishment in 1978.

the use of SCBA with improved protective gear are examples of changes that have reduced injuries and saved the lives of firefighters. Breaking down racial and gender barriers made the job a reality for many people. But the fire service has never been quick to accept change. In fact, many close to the fire service believe that certain changes in the fire service require a generation, or about 20 years, before they are accepted.

### Training

Another element in the all-important aspect fostering the brotherhood among firefighters is the ongoing training members complete. Crews often train together so that they build reliance on one another in live situations. There are several instructional methods available to firefighters, all of which are part of a complete training program. Classroom studying with books, notes, and a blackboard similar to any type of schooling is one form of firefighter training. This training can encompass anything from the mundane basics of fire science to highly intensive understanding of new equipment and trends.

Attending local, regional, or national seminars that include firefighters from different departments is another type of formal training. These seminars generally offer classes on specific topics that can be extremely in-depth, allowing firefighters to hone specific skills. Seminars also include discussion groups that may include a panel of experts from around the world who share their knowledge through an open forum. Manufacturers also get involved with seminars and trade

A fire instructor takes a break from the intense heat within the training center as he oversees controlled room and contents fires for new recruits. Those that teach when they are not assigned to a firehouse maintain a second set of turnout gear for training. The fires that trainers use to teach will tear up gear because of the constant and intense environments that they're in. Fire service tradition dictates that well-worn active duty gear be broken in with actual fires instead of training fires.

shows to educate firefighters or instructors on new tools and techniques that they would like to promote to the fire service. They hope that the attendees will return home with a new-found need for these products and purchase them in the near future.

Controlled hands-on situations are another way firefighters improve their skills using hand tools, fire extinguishers, rescue techniques, and fire suppression methods. Training academies are available either within a department, through neighboring departments, or from special schools that offer fire-resistant buildings where controlled burns can be setup, offering live fire, smoke, and heat. These fires don't go out unless the participants actually extinguish them with water or foam.

Some of these structures can be altered with doors so that each time firefighters train they have different obstacles to overcome. This type of facility also will have multistory structures enabling crews to practice ladder work, climb both interior and exterior stairs, conduct multifloor searches, or rescue trapped victims. Heavy dummies that come in many sizes are used to represent victims who need to be found.

The other training experience that was once considerably more prevalent was the opportunity to conduct real fire and searches in actual buildings and residential dwellings that would sustain genuine structural damage. Buildings that were being condemned often were made available to the fire department, as well as structures that were to be torn down for new buildings. In some areas, homeowners would donate an old building to the fire department which would then use the structure for live training before burning it to the ground, saving the owner the expense of having to pay the costs of demolition.

But this practice has been greatly curtailed for several reasons. First and foremost, it was discontinued because of the potential negative

Firefighters at a training facility descend the interior stairs with an attack line to hit a basement fire in a room that was specially designed to retain the maximum amount of heat. This feature of the room provides a real incentive to find the fire and put it out quickly.

environmental impact of the burn, which degraded air quality. Second, and of equal significance, is that many old buildings contained asbestos, a cancer-causing material that was hazardous to firefighters' health. So today, unless the dwelling receives a clear notice that there was no asbestos used in its construction or that the asbestos has been properly removed, fire departments will not put firefighters in the position of risking exposure. Finally, with the expansion and growth of urban and suburban areas, the possibility, however remote, of damaging neighboring properties with an intentionally set fire is too great a liability for most fire departments to assume.

As the frequency of working structure fires decreases, the importance of seasoned firefighters sharing their prior battle experience with new recruits, taking part in mock drills, and fighting contained burns becomes increasingly more important in the training process. After all, some firefighters may rarely encounter a bonafide structure fire, and may only experience staged fires making the mix of official textbook instruction with real-life experience—both successful and unsuccessful—the most beneficial.

## On the Job

The brotherhood between firefighters extends well beyond the duties and responsibilities of mentoring and training, and living and eating with one another. They have to trust each other every day in situations that could endanger their lives or those of innocent citizens. Each time the alarm sounds and they leave quarters en route to an emergency, there is a distinct possibility that some or all of the firefighters will never return. Every month, firefighters lose their lives in the line of duty. Nearly 100 firefighters died in 2002. As they train together, it is imperative that firefighters learn to trust each other and come to understand that if the life of a firefighter is on the

Firefighters from Rescue 5 in New York use a stokes basket to carry the equipment that they need inside this building. FDNY allows summer uniforms to include short pants, though it is up to the discretion of each firefighter as to what is worn. But the rigging harness and radio shown are part of the required gear for this particular assignment.

line, their brothers and sisters will not be far away and will stop at nothing, including imperiling their own lives, to save those in trouble.

A situation in which firefighters risked their lives to save their brothers tragically occurred on December 3, 1999, when two seasoned and dedicated firefighters became disoriented and lost in a warehouse fire in Worcester, Massachusetts. As the distress call was given from these firefighters, many others were sent to their aid, none of them knowing the exact position of those who were trapped. The fire, smoke, and heat were intense, yet the difficult conditions did not stop the other firefighters from trying to save their brothers. Sadly, the trapped firefighters were not found, and four of the rescuers themselves became disoriented and trapped, resulting in the deaths of six firefighters. Each firefighter who went to the aid of the first two went willingly, unselfishly, and without hesitation. After the four rescuers were missing, the chief officer on the scene had to forcefully stop additional firefighters from going in, all of whom felt a sense of guilt and betrayal for not being able to save their brothers.

Those that perished were firefighters Paul Brotherton and Jerry Lucey, who were in trouble initially, while firefighters Tim Jackson, Jay Lyons, Joe McGuirk, and Lieutenant Tom Spencer made the ultimate sacrifice attempting to aid their brothers. But the bonds of brotherhood carry on in the Worcester Fire Department, as several surviving members of the tragedy have stepped in to help the wives and children of those who perished.

Upon making sure that all of the recruits have exited, the fire department instructor is the last one to leave the heat trailer.

In addition to dedicating themselves to the safety of members of their own companies, firefighters back each other up when multiple alarms deplete companies from one department or from an area within a large department. The backup companies cover the response districts of those that are busy, and the duties and responsibilities of the change companies (those that move to different quarters) vary depending on the sense of duty and tradition that the these firefighters have.

A rookie exits a modified steel container that was originally used to transport goods overseas. The container is now part of the training facility for firefighters in Austin, Texas, and provides an environment that retains a tremendous amount of heat. Rookies exit the container when they can no longer take the heat or when their air cylinders signal low air.

After removing the regulator from his mask, a firefighter in a well-smoked helmet with a melted plastic shield discusses the adventure. One thing that is stressed while recruits are in the training container is that they are not alone and that they should rely on their fellow firefighters in the event that they need help.

When the local company members return from a fire, oftentimes they are in need of a change of clothes or a shower. They also may need to change out some of the equipment on their rig so that they can get back into service for another run. Some change companies will leave as soon as they are released, while others will wait to see how they can help get the other firefighters back in service. Often engine companies that have used large amounts of hose at a fire may have to switch out the wet hose for dry hose or simply repack their hose beds if they weren't able to do so at the scene.

The change company will offer to help with this changeover, but some companies have a tradition that no outside firefighters are allowed to pack, or bend, their hose. Bending is a term for packing the hose bed, which requires hose to be laid out and curved back and forth so that it comes out properly when it's pulled off at a fire. In this case, the change company members assist by laying out the hose on the floor, connecting the couplings, and hoisting it up to the hose bed, letting the engine company take it from there.

## Off the Job

Even off duty, the brotherhood continues for many firefighters who share side jobs, sports interests, and friendships together. Families of firefighters that are not related are often friends and get together socially. Picnics, volleyball, bowling tournaments, and softball games are a few of the traditional activities that more departments are now reviving as they try to promote the unity between fire department families with firefighters' personal families. However, in some cases the brotherhood can have a detrimental effect on personal relationships that do not center on the fire service. For instance, a spouse can feel left out or threatened by the close-knit nature of the firefighting lifestyle.

Firefighters often work together to support charitable causes, especially those charities that work with children. Each summer, firefighters sponsor and run camps, which include counseling, for child burn victims. These camps provide children with a place to come and be among others that share the same concerns and worries in an environment where no one is self-conscious

Training is an integral component of every fire department. These firefighters and officers represent the Fowlerville Volunteer Fire Department in Michigan. They are posing for a traditional group photo at the site where they burned down an abandoned house as part of a training session.

of their injuries, allowing them to function without any inhibitions. Another area of great pleasure to firefighters involves charitable programs that lead up to the holidays. Many a Christmas, Santa Claus has arrived on a fire truck to the delight of the waiting children. The departments collect toys for the Toys for Tots program so that these needy children are ensured a gift.

Another popular charity drive that firefighters participate in is a fill-the-boot campaign. Positioning themselves at the corners of busy intersections and carrying a fireboot in hand, firefighters have passing motorists fill the boots with donations to raise money for causes such as the Muscular Dystrophy Association (MDA) or to help widows and orphans of fallen firefighters. Examples of

As fire blows out the front door over the heads of these two firefighters, they stand ready with a backup line to intervene for the crew that is entering this training fire from the rear of the building. The fire department received permission to conduct room fires in this abandoned house in North Carolina before burning the house to the foundation for the homeowner.

dedicated efforts in fill-the-boot collection drives include that of the Fairfax County, Virginia, firefighters from station 38 who in 2002 raised $21,000 for the MDA in a four-day period. That drive was recognized as exceptional by the MDA. Also, firefighters from the city of Houston raised $391,000 in 2002, and have broken donation records for four of the past five years. This was just part of the more than $18 milion collected by the International Association of Firefighters and other fire service affiliations on behalf of the MDA in 2002. Along with raising funds for the the MDA, many firefighters volunteer at the association's summer camps for children with muscular dystrophy. In fact, firefighters represent the single largest source of volunteers for these 100 or so camps that are run across the country each summer.

During a training rotation involving nozzle work, a chief officer advises the pipe man before he opens the tip. They take a moment to observe the behavior of the fire that is climbing the rear wall and beginning to bank off the ceiling toward them. The walls of this training center are lined with a special type of heat-resistant tile to preserve the integrity of the building for repeated burns as well as retain the maximum amount of heat to provide a challenging environment for firefighters. The yellow box that is visible in the foreground on the SCBA belt of the chief is a PASS. This is a safety device that emits a piercing sound if the firefighter remains motionless for a designated period of time. It is intended to be a locator for trapped or incapacitated firefighters.

# CHAPTER 4
# The Action

Prior to the implementation of SCBAs, firefighters entered a fire building with nothing to protect them from inhaling smoke, noxious gases, and chemicals that were emitted from burning debris. Here, three firefighters assist the nozzle man with a 2 1/2-inch line while another stands ready with a pike pole to separate debris so they can hit any remaining hot spots.

Although the dangers associated with hazardous materials have become considerably more prevalent in recent years, they have always been part of the job for firefighters. Fortunately, technology has greatly increased the levels of protection available to the firefighters who have to deal with hazardous chemicals. In 1978, this was representative of an entry suit used by Chicago's Snorkel Squad 1. One firefighter is shown assisting another into the rubber suit that was used over and over again after being rinsed off. Unlike modern suits, the breathing hose then was on the outside of the suit and not protected from the dangers of corrosive agents. Today, many suits are used only once before being discarded.

**Anthrax**

In response to the fear of anthrax poisoning during 2002, multiple reports of suspicious white powders, especially in large cities and communities, came into many fire departments. Although most cases were false alarms or hoaxes, the deadly potential of anthrax being present required diligence in evaluating each encounter. Routines were established based on the level of threat and danger and, with few exceptions nationally, there was little cause for alarm.

One suburban fire department responded to a report of a threatening letter with a suspicious white powder. Because of the letter's wording and the establishment it targeted, the letter was considered a serious threat. The fire department had never really expected a situation like this to happen, but its members investigated the scene and tested the substance before notifying the

**P**erhaps not every firefighter has been in a situation that was frightening or that spurred thoughts of imminent danger or death, but many have. And it doesn't have to be a raging fire to have caused concern. The following real-life encounters detail tough, frightening, disappointing, proud, or particularly rewarding days on the job for the firefighters who lived them.

On the fireground, everyone works together. The pump operator here is busy attaching another large diameter line to the engine as other firefighters remove the necessary lengths of hose from the hose bed.

Car fires present a significant number of responses for many fire departments. Most car fires under the hood are electrical in nature while fires in other parts of the cars are often intentionally set. Firefighters are cautious of introducing oxygen to the fire when they pry open the hood of the car thereby causing flare-ups. Here, California Department of Forestry (CDF) and San Bernardino firefighters attack a car fire in the middle of a busy street. As other firefighters approach to offer assistance, one firefighter is prying up a corner of the hood while another gets water on the fire. They won't be able to release the hood latch while the engine compartment is on fire.

postal authorities and the FBI. Prior to handling this investigation, the fire department obtained various testing materials so that it could determine whether the substance was truly a deadly poison that could kill an individual or cause serious illness through the minutest contact. After all, the first domestic contact with anthrax was determined to be via a trace amount on a computer keyboard that poisoned and killed the person who had used the workstation.

The hazardous materials, or hazmat, team who responded to this anthrax call consisted of three firefighters, all of whom were wearing the appropriate level protective suits. Two of these hazmat technicians entered the building where the suspicious letter was received, while the third remained at the door for support. Upon encountering the unknown powder, one technician administered the test, waiting for a certain reaction to occur and a specific color change in the testing material. To the dread of the two techs, the test result was positive. They looked at one another with fear before calmly re-administering the test to check for accuracy.

When the second test also returned a positive finding, they met eyes with the support tech who immediately understood the significance of what had just happened. After performing the same test many times prior and coming up with negative results, the firefighters began to fear for the unknown. They wondered about the employees who did not have the benefit of a protective chemical suit and had been totally unsuspecting of coming into contact with something so potentially deadly when they got up that morning and went to work.

As the firefighters began the task of isolating the powder and containing it for federal officials, others were busy quarantining the office workers. The police stretched the ominous yellow scene tape to seal off the area and create a hot zone perimeter so that no one was allowed to enter without protective suits.

Upon completion of the investigation and turning over the powder to the FBI, the firefighters thought about their mortality, the unknown, their families, and how the job had changed from the time they had signed on. Raging fires, building collapses, vehicle wrecks, and industrial accidents were all dangerous incidents that the seasoned firefighters had encountered numerous times in the past. However, none presented the same kind of danger as an anthrax attack, where firefighters had little control of the outcome. Further testing by the FBI negated the results of the on-scene testing and determined the powder to be harmless. The firefighters were very relieved, yet they maintained a sense of fear about coming in contact with more unknown biological threats in the future.

## Making a Poor Assumption

Sometimes being scared on the job doesn't have anything to do with being in trouble yourself. When career firefighters in a large community responded to what should have been a routine fire in an upscale, two-story house, they found that they would not leave before learning a valuable lesson. The fire was on the second floor, and by the time the squad company arrived, the engine company was making an aggressive interior attack and the truck company was ventilating.

The squad company assumed the other companies had made a primary search to see if the home's residents, whose whereabouts were unknown, were trapped in the blaze. As the squad company pushed its way past the engine

Two firefighters at a "still and box" (a local fire that has escalated) alarm in a two-flat residential building in Chicago need some fresh air after knocking down the fire. All of the front windows have been ventilated to allow the smoke, heat, and noxious gases to escape so the engine company can work inside attacking the fire while the truck company searches for victims. The large 2 1/2-inch attack line is quite heavy and cumbersome going up the stairs to the second floor.

This pumper operator has his hands full at the hydrant, managing several lines off at this fire. The rest of his company is at the fire building and they maintain radio contact so that he can properly manage the water pressure for the attack lines that are in use.

crew and the hose line going up the narrow stairs, the company encountered intense heat conditions at the top of the stairs. The squad members quickly checked the rooms on one side of the second floor for trapped victims, but they then decided not to push past the nozzle for fear of the attic collapsing and isolating them from the others. Instead, they entered a room on the other side of the hallway and encountered members of the truck company pulling ceiling, looking for the fire above. Assuming that the balance of the rooms had been cleared since the truck company was on-scene first and was now pulling ceiling, the squad members assisted with the ceiling duty. Then they noticed that the truck company was gone and they were unsure if one additional room that was beyond the nozzle had been searched. When the squad company reached the room in question, they saw another crew pulling an unconscious victim from the room.

The squad company members quickly realized the mistake, knowing that instead of pulling ceiling, they could have pushed beyond the nozzle and possibly saved the life of the victim who ended up dying several days later. After the fire, the squad company couldn't help but relive the incident and pass on to others the importance of relying on their training without making uninformed assumptions.

### Firefighters in Trouble

Embarking on a mission to find fellow firefighters who have gone missing can test even the most seasoned firefighters. Late one winter evening, fire broke out in the basement of a two-and-a half story, masonry commercial building. The business where the fire originated was a printing company with various flammable chemicals and liquids present. When the first units arrived and saw that the building was well involved, they immediately requested additional assistance by initiating an extra alarm. Upon arrival minutes later, the company officer of the rescue squad heard fireground radio chatter about firefighters a half-story underground on the lower level who were in trouble. He ordered his driver to set up in front of the building and to use the full amount of scene lighting that was mounted to the rig. He hoped that the light would be visible through the windows to the company inside and might help the members find their way out.

After donning air packs and receiving clearance to initiate a search and rescue, the squad company followed two hand lines, one of which was charged with water, down the stairs. There the company found the other firefighters' nozzles on the floor. The group thought that three firefighters had entered the basement but was not sure. The squad company then found tools and a hand light on the floor and tried counting the items in an effort to determine how many firefighters had come before them. The squad company picked up the charged line and separated into two teams; one started attacking the fire and providing backup while the other began a search. The firefighters were able to knock down the heaviest fire but were unable to locate the missing firefighters who had subsequently made it out safely on their own through a different entrance.

Taking the opportunity to gain knowledge from the incident, the squad company realized that although what they had done was sound

A tired Chicago firefighter rests on the outrigger of an E-ONE aerial at the scene of an extra alarm fire. Standard issue turnout gear in Chicago consists of the three-quarter hip boots, a long coat, and a traditional-style helmet.

tactically, in the future, they should take an extra minute to determine exactly how many people were missing and who they were. This would eliminate any potential confusion that might occur if the squad company would have come upon firefighters other than those who they were looking for, perhaps other firefighters who were also looking for the lost company.

### First Flashover

A flashover occurs when the heat generated by a fire radiates to other combustable materials around it until they reach their ignition point and burst into flames. The first time that a firefighter experiences a flashover or backdraft is both dramatic and terrifying due to the extreme nature of the events, combined with the incredible speed with which they occur and then disappear. Such was the case for a truck officer and a partner who were conducting a search for victims. They were not accompanied by a hose line and, after they had opened the door to a room and pushed several feet inside, it flashed. It was over before they even had a chance to react. What the officer remembered about the incident is that the fire raced around all of the walls, beginning at one side and traveled to each successive wall faster than he could watch it. Instinctively, he and his partner backed out of the room and closed the door until they could re-enter with a hose to knock down the fire. The unnerving encounter, which happened many years ago, is still a vivid memory for him and for his partner.

### Firefighter Down

Church fires are notoriously difficult to fight when they are able to get a good start ahead of the fire department. The vaulted ceilings create a dangerous interior environment because the roof can collapse quickly. This nightmare came true late one very cold evening when fire erupted in an old church. As the chief officer on-scene feared, part of the church collapsed before all the firefighters could evacuate. Ten to 15 firefighters managed to escape, but one firefighter was not present for roll call. Initial media reports stated the number of trapped firefighters to be five or six. After the initial shock of the event, firefighters were sent to search for their missing brother. However, one company officer, to the surprise of his crew, lead them to a nearby store to call their spouses first, knowing that they would not be relieved until morning and wanting to relieve fears generated by the erroneous media reports.

When the firefighters resumed searching for the missing firefighter, they had to work under one remaining wall that had not fallen, as other firefighters used an aerial device in an attempt to knock down the wall away from where the firefighters were working. Sadly, the firefighters did not recover the body of their fallen brother until the next morning.

### Even When You Do It By the Book

The challenges firefighters face cannot always be solved simply by following proper protocol and procedures. Pulling up to a bungalow late at night

Overhaul is the responsibility of the truck company. This job is accomplished by removing walls, ceilings, and debris to make sure that there are no hidden hot spots of fire while the engine company stands by with a charged line. The truckies often have the dirty faces because they're the ones looking up while pulling down ceilings with a pike pole. This firefighter's coat is wet and covered with bits and pieces of paint and plaster.

A multitude of hoses crisscross the street in front of this stubborn 5-11 alarm fire in downtown Chicago. Fire-fighters in the foreground are manning a multiversal gun in preparations of attacking this fire. Before they open the nozzle, they will need an all clear signifying that firefighters on the fire escape and inside the building are safely out of the way. The firefighters at both ends of the fire escape demonstrate a vulnerability that existed prior to the use of fire-resistant hoods. They are wearing protective coats, boots, gloves, helmets, and breathing apparatus, but their ears, necks, and faces outside the mask are fully exposed to heat and fire.

with fire showing from the front should have been routine. Because no one outside of the building could confirm whether anyone was still inside, the squad company made its way to the rear to make entry. Once in back, the firefighters encountered steel scissor gates that were barring entrance to the back door. The gates were reinforced with 2x4s that were protecting the home from intruders in this less-than-ideal neighborhood.

As two firefighters began cutting the gates, the squad officer breached a nearby wall and broke right into a bedroom. As they passed through the bedroom, the firefighters conducted a search and found no victims. Upon exiting the bedroom, they could see the fire at the end of the hall. Their training taught them to begin their search in the rooms nearest to the source of the fire, due to the fact that victims in those rooms would have the greatest risk of danger.

In doing so, they passed another bedroom which was immediately adjacent to the room that they had entered, but in the opposite direction of the fire. After searching the other rooms and making their way back to the end of the hallway, they discovered six children in the last room. All of the children were unconscious and unable to be revived. While the firefighters knew they had done the search in textbook fashion, they could not help but ponder what would have happened if they would have searched the bedroom where the children were first. Could those crucial few minutes had made a difference for any or all of those kids? This thought would live with the fire-fighters for their entire career. So did the fact that many neighbors blamed the rescuers for the children's deaths and threw debris at them as they removed the children's bodies, which made the gruesome task even more difficult.

All of the protective clothing that firefighters wear today can have detrimental side effects when the weather is extremely hot and humid. As the gear encapsulates a firefighter keeping them safe from the fire, it also retains body heat and inhibits the escape of moisture. Here, a firefighter is taking advantage of the loose spray from a fire hydrant to cool down from the summer heat and rinse the smoke from his eyes. He has his boots rolled down as an added means of keeping cool.

A multitude of rescue tools are being deployed or are ready to be used including air bags, hydraulic tools, and wood cribbing at this rollover accident with a trapped victim. Cribbing is used to stabilize the vehicle from moving. The air bag was flat when it was inserted underneath the door and subsequently inflated with air to lift the truck. This is one means of providing access to the driver.

## Sometimes the Best Tool is Good Luck

Extensive training, good equipment, and staying focused are only three of the elements that a firefighter needs to be successful. Several years ago in the middle of the night, multiple companies responded to a fire in a six-story commercial building of mill construction that measured approximately 300x125 feet. Upon arrival the firefighters encountered heavy smoke pushing out of all the windows with no visible fire. While extra alarms were sounded for additional companies, one of the companies took a two-and-a half-inch line into the basement to find the fire. They were met by intense heat and were unable to locate any fire before they needed to go back outside and switch out their air bottles. In the meantime, a chief had decided to set up a multiversal—a portable deluge gun that is capable of being fed by several attack lines at the same time—in front of an overhead door to direct water into the building once the door was opened.

As the company officer was getting a spare bottle from his rig, a backdraft ignited and the whole building flashed. Now instead of smoke, heavy fire was venting from every window. The explosion was so intense that the officer had to duck under the rig as bricks began to rain down over the entire fireground. His first inclination was to look for his company, the firefighters he worked with and lived with each duty day. Upon finding them unharmed, he and his crew looked around to see what other firefighters they could help.

What they saw was incredible. The firefighters who had been standing directly in front of the building to put the multiversal to use were surrounded by debris piled everywhere. The scene was as if they were standing on an island in the middle of all the chaos. As the walls of the building collapsed, the steel frame around the overhead door they were standing close to came down around them and provided a protective barrier, saving their lives.

Firefighters make final adjustments as a hose line is charged and they prepare to attack this house fire on Chicago's south side. Each is equipped with a SCBA. The nozzle man has chosen to lower the plastic face shield on his helmet to protect him from debris. But unlike the other two firefighters, he did not pull his boots up to protect his pants.

As it turned out, someone had forced open a rear door to the alley, which provided a fresh influx of oxygen into the building. Firefighters in a rear stairwell where the door was opened were protected by the concrete-encased construction of the stairwell. The force was so intense that it blew the leather helmets right off the heads of several firefighters. While many firefighters sustained varying injuries and several rigs were damaged, no one sustained any job-ending injuries that night.

## Getting Burned

Focusing on the job at hand and the dedication required in doing so is what contributes to a great firefighter. Upon arriving at a well involved fire, firefighters on the rescue squad who were responsible for providing backup were informed of a firefighter who was in trouble. His face piece had somehow come apart and he was disoriented.

As two firefighters began their search, they kept low under the dense smoke that was banking down toward the floor. The heat was intense and companies were having water problems, so the searchers were without the safety of a hose line. Fully encapsulated in their turnout gear with air packs, they felt the incredible heat and felt the fire was close to the flash point. The heat came down so fast that it forced the lead man to the floor immediately.

Conditions were deteriorating quickly and the lead man was convinced the room would flash. He also knew that he was heating up badly. He lost his helmet and felt a searing pain on his lower back, on the top of his head, and around the seal of his mask. But he and his partner were able to meet up with the disoriented firefighter

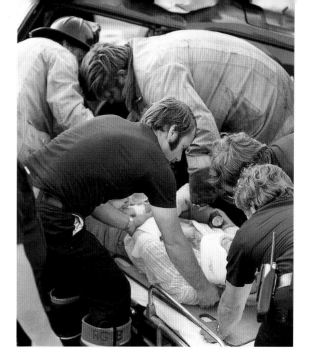

In the early 1980s, when the concept of on-scene advanced life support was in its infancy, concerns about blood-born pathogens were not an issue. In this image, EMS workers and firefighters are lacking the most basic of protection tools that are utilized today—latex gloves.

and together make their way out of the building. Once outside, the lead firefighter discovered that he did in fact sustain burns to the top of his head and on his face around the seal of his mask. For some reason his bunker coat had bunched up on his SCBA harness, which allowed some exposure and subsequent burns to his lower back around the waistline of the pants. Even though he knew he was injured, his perseverance and the drive to come to the aid of a brother had enabled him to continue the search.

As two firefighters in the bucket direct the elevated master stream at the fire from above, two others confer about other equipment that they need off the truck with the rig's driver, who is stationed at the turntable.

# AFTERWORD
## FDNY–Still the
## Greatest Job in the World

A night tour of Rescue 1 with tools in hand poses by their new rig after being released from a job. From left to right they are firefighters Michael Sullivan, Shawn Ashe, Sean Nealon, Jason Faso, Anthony Tedeschi, and Lieutenant Tony Tarabocchia. The rig, a 2002 Saulsbury rescue on an E-ONE chassis was dontated to the FDNY by Airbus, and dedicated to the memory of the fallen firefighters that died at the World Trade Center on September 11, 2001. Partially visible below the windshield is the word 'outstanding', which was a frequent response of the late Captain Terry Hatton who was one of the principle designers of the new vehicle.

Firefighter Kevin Kroth, a 15-year FDNY veteran with seven years on Rescue 1, stands by as engine and truck company crews investigate an alarm. His leather helmet shows the tell-tale signs of encountering a great amount of heat and fire over the course of his tenure with this company.

There is no doubt that firefighters are placed in life-threatening situations on a regular basis. If they dwell on the possibility of serious injury or death, it will adversely affect their ability to perform the job. If they ignore the possibility, they may get sloppy and unnecessarily put themselves in danger.

Whether in New York or elsewhere, these factors do not detract those who are committed to working as firefighters. They love the camaraderie and great work environment resulting from being part of a tight-knit group of individuals working and living together. Although firefighting may draw people from all walks of life, they all get along well together and bond like a close family. There is also a mutual respect that exists between the bosses and rank-in-file since the bosses have been promoted up through the ranks and have not forgotten what it's like to be a firefighter. The bosses remember being above a fire, on a line, or conducting a search, which helps to keep the group tight. Firefighters know that few people can go to work for such long hours and actually enjoy what they do, who they work with, and be eager for their next tour of duty.

But there is a flip side—the worst part of the job. Aside from the heartache and misery that comes to the citizens that they help and protect, comes a firefighter's realization that good friends die doing this job. In all departments, a single firefighter death greatly impacts many people. Thoughts about having worked with someone so closely, having responded to the

Firefighters Shawn Ashe and Jason Faso are prepared to go to work if called upon by the chief. Ashe's position on this tour includes the irons and Faso is responsible for the can, a water-filled fire extinguisher that is used for small fires. They stand ready with SCBA, hoods, gloves, flashlights, and hand tools. They are positioned in front of their rig where they can access additional tools and equipment if called to do so.

fatal incident together, or of having had morning coffee together the day of the tragedy are extremely difficult to bear within such a close-knit community. In 2001, 343 New York City firefighters and one member of the fire patrol died during the World Trade Center terrorist attacks. The impact of this devastating blow to the FDNY family was greater than anything else it has ever had to deal with. The entire world grieved the loss of these heroes who unselfishly, without thought for their own safety, went to the aid of several thousand civilians who needed to be evacuated from the twin towers. These same civilians relied on the firefighters to extinguish the massive fires that threatened others. Despite the loss of their fellow firefighters, the grief-stricken members of the FDNY could not and did not stop performing their vital duties at the trade center and throughout the rest of the five boroughs of New York City that day or in the ensuing days and weeks.

In an outpouring of support and in the true spirit of the brotherhood, firefighters from nearby towns and cities in New York, from neighboring states and from around the country went to New York offering aid and solace. They worked at the Trade Center site when needed and occupied New York City firehouses to protect the city so that FDNY firefighters could work at Ground Zero, hoping to find those who had been trapped and honor their memories. From September 11 until the recovery effort was complete some nine months later, there was not a single moment at Ground Zero without an FDNY presence. The New York firefighters never left alone any of their fallen. For one firefighter, probably the most rewarding experience during his 12 years with the FDNY he said was being part of the crew that helped to dig out a Port Authority police officer from the trade center rubble. Sadly, this was one of only a small number of survivors that were found.

Al Benjamin has spent 13 of his 25 years as an FDNY firefighter assigned to Rescue 1 in Manhattan. Here, he awaits instructions from the chief while on scene at a small roof fire in a three-flat walk-up. His SCBA regulator is visible hanging on his right, and he has a flashlight and portable radio microphone on his left side.

As horrific and tragic as the devastation and loss at the World Trade Center was though, it cannot be allowed to overshadow the fact that in 2001 six other FDNY firefighters gave their lives in the line of duty at other incidents. These men and women, along with many others who are represented by statistics mentioned elsewhere in this book, gave unselfishly of themselves and have each created a missing thread in the fabric that is the fire service. However, the bonds of the fire service, its culture, and traditions are strong enough to keep this fabric from coming apart. Thankfully, no FDNY firefighters lost their lives in the line of duty in 2002.

Each and every day before and since September 11, the members of the FDNY who were on the job prior, as well as those who jumped at the opportunity to join the ranks of the largest fire department in the world after 9-11, report for duty twice a day and are proud to be a part of the greatest job in the world.

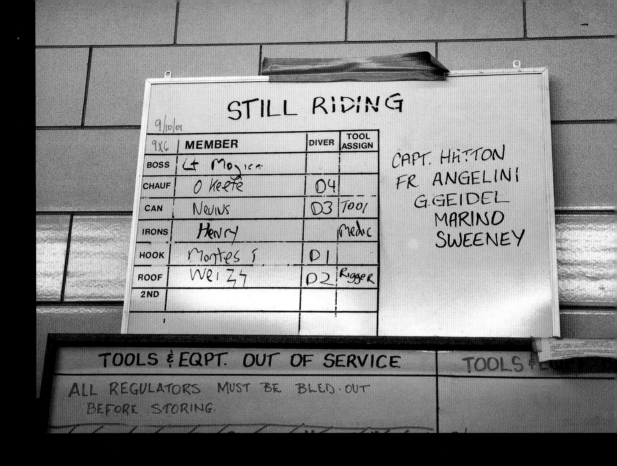

STILL RIDING

9/10/01

| 9XC | MEMBER | DIVER | TOOL ASSIGN |
|------|--------|-------|-------------|
| BOSS | Lt Mojica | | |
| CHAUF | O'Keefe | D4 | |
| CAN | Nevins | D3 | Tool |
| IRONS | Henry | | Medic |
| HOOK | Montesi | D1 | |
| ROOF | Weiss | D2 | Rigger |
| 2ND | | | |

CAPT. HATTON
FR. ANGELINI
G. GEIDEL
MARINO
SWEENEY

TOOLS & EQPT. OUT OF SERVICE          TOOLS

ALL REGULATORS MUST BE BLED·OUT
BEFORE STORING.

On September 10, 2001, the riding assignment for the night tour of FDNY Rescue 1 was written on the dry-erase board that hung in the apparatus bay, just like it was on every other day. Each name was placed in riding order with designations for each job and specialty. These five firefighters and the company officer were finishing their tour when an airplane smashed into the north tower of the World Trade Center at 8:45 a.m. on September 11. The morning relief tour, which consisted of four firefighters and the captain, had already arrived, and both crews responded to the emergency in lower Manhattan. Tragically, these 11 members perished along with 332 other members of the FDNY when the Twin Towers collapsed. This board remains in the quarters of Rescue 1 as a tribute to those who responded that morning and never returned. Captain Terry S. Hatton, Lieutenant Dennis Mojica, and firefighters Joseph Angelini Sr., Gary Geidel, William Henry, Kenneth Marino, Michael Montesi, Gerard Nevins, Patrick O'Keefe, Brian Sweeney, and David Weiss all lost their lives

# INDEX

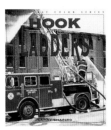

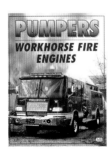